Jan   242.642
13.99   SWA

SEP   2012

MAN DOES
NOT LIVE BY
SPORTS ALONE

D0067709

MAN DOES NOT LIVE BY SPORTS ALONE

devotions for men

HOWARD BOOKS
A DIVISION OF SIMON & SCHUSTER
New York   London   Toronto   Sydney

DR. DENNIS SWANBERG

- *Increase* faith in the hearts of growing Christians
- *Inspire* holiness in the lives of believers
- *Instill* hope in the hearts of struggling people everywhere

Because He's coming again!

Howard Books, a division of Simon & Schuster, Inc.
1230 Avenue of the Americas, New York, NY 10020
www.howardpublishing.com

HOWARD
BOOKS

Man Does Not Live by Sports Alone © 2006 Dennis Swanberg

13 Digit ISBN: 978-1-4165-3593-5

10 9 8 7 6 5 4 3 2 1

HOWARD is a registered trademark of Simon & Schuster, Inc.

Manufactured in the United States

For information regarding special discounts for bulk purchases, please contact Simon & Schuster Special Sales at 1-800-456-6798 or business@simonandschuster.com.

Edited by Between the Lines
Cover design by John Lucas
Interior design by John Mark Luke Designs
Photos from Photos.com

Scripture quotations marked CEV are from the *Contemporary English Version*, copyright © 1995 by American Bible Society. Used by permission. Scripture quotations marked HCSB are from the *Holman Christian Standard Bible®*, copyright © 1999, 2000, 2002, 2003 by Holman Bible Publishers. Used by permission. Scripture quotations marked MSG are taken from *The Message*. Copyright © 1993, 1994, 1995, 1996, 2000, 2001, 2002. Used by permission of NavPress Publishing Group. Scripture quotations marked NASB are taken from the *New American Standard Bible®*. © 1960, 1962, 1963, 1968, 1971, 1972, 1973, 1975, 1977, 1995 by The Lockman Foundation. Used by permission. Scripture quotations marked NCV are from the *Holy Bible, New Century Version®*. Copyright © 1987, 1988, 1991 by Thomas Nelson, Inc. Used by permission. All rights reserved. Scripture quotations marked NIV are from the *Holy Bible, New International Version®*. Copyright © 1973, 1978, 1984 by International Bible Society. Used by permission of Zondervan. All rights reserved. Scripture quotations marked NKJV are from the *New King James Version*. Copyright © 1982, 1988 by Thomas Nelson, Inc. All rights reserved. Scripture quotations marked NLT are from the *Holy Bible, New Living Translation*, copyright © 1996. Used by permission of Tyndale House Publishers, Inc., Wheaton, Illinois 60189. All rights reserved. Scripture quotations marked TLB are taken from *The Living Bible*, copyright © 1971. Used by permission of Tyndale House Publishers, Inc., Wheaton, Illinois 60189. All rights reserved.

contents

contents

introduction

OK, FELLAS, this book's for you. And it's about time. After all, the women have had their fair share of books for years—and you know exactly the kind of "girl books" I'm talking about: all those frilly tomes with flowers and babies and hearts and kittens on the covers. But where have they been hiding all the books for us guys—those of us who, when we're finished with our daily devotional time, would rather read the sports page than the fashion page? Well, boys, here it is.

This book is designed specifically for all you manly men who love sports. You know who you are: you're the guys who'd rather talk about Peyton Manning and Kurt Schilling than Hillary and Bill. You have informed opinions about who's the best receiver in the NFL, the best arm in the Majors, and the best 2-guard in the NBA. You know the NASCAR drivers by their names and their numbers. And even though you probably can't name three or four of the nine Supreme Court justices, you can name all nine starters for the Atlanta Braves. Yep, when it comes to the sports bug, you've got it bad.

But you're also the men who try to spend at least a few minutes every day reading your Bible and getting your plays called by the Coach upstairs. So, hopefully, this book will give you and your sports-minded buddies a few ideas to chew on and a few things to talk about. Because this book isn't just about guy stuff; it's about guy stuff and God stuff (with a strong emphasis on the latter).

The guy stuff you and your peeps like to chew the fat about isn't a deep, dark mystery; it usually fits into a few major categories: sports, business, politics, cars, money, the yard, more sports, your fantasy league, and did I say sports? The God stuff, on the other hand, may be a little more difficult to categorize. And that's where this book can help. I've divided it into thirty personal devotional readings that can double as jumping-off points for discussions with your friends about God's playbook.

So take a tip from your ol' pal Dennis Swanberg (known to my friends, and now you, as "the Swan"). The next time you roll out of bed and head down to the local diner for an early-morning confab with the boys—or the next time you do lunch with the guys just so you can talk about matters of life and sports—remember that it's not enough to be a manly man who talks about manly stuff. You've also got to be a godly man who talks—and thinks—about God stuff. When you do, you'll be a winner in the game of life . . . and you'll be invited to the postgame celebration that endures for all eternity.

WHATEVER YOU
LOVE MOST, BE IT SPORTS,
PLEASURE, BUSINESS OR GOD,
THAT IS YOUR GOD.

Billy Graham

A WORD FROM THE COACH

You shall have no other gods before me.

—Exodus 20:3 NIV

THE CAPTAIN OF YOUR TEAM

WARMUPS

- Who's the captain of your team?
- Who's calling the plays?
- In other words, who's really running things at your house: you, your wife, the kids, the neighbors, your cat Mittens . . . or God?

GOING DEEP

IT'S EASY to talk about letting God take charge of your life, but how do you actually manage to do it? After all, you're a busy man with tons of responsibilities. You've got important decisions to make *every day*, and you can't wait for God to carve the answers on a stone tablet, Ten Commandments style. Sometimes you've got to make decisions *right now* or suffer the consequences.

> HE WHO OFFERS TO GOD A SECOND PLACE OFFERS HIM NO PLACE.
>
> *John Ruskin*

And as you know, play calling isn't always simple. It isn't like you get to make decisions in a vacuum. Far from it! If you're married, you probably consult your wife; if you've got kids, you've got to think about them too. Your boss may have a little something to say about things. And if you're a dues-paying member of the A-Team (that's America's Team), then your good ol' Uncle Sam has a few rules you need to follow as well. So where exactly does God fit into this picture? Well, here's the way it is: either you manage to put your heavenly Father in first place, or he doesn't really fit in at all.

If you insist on relegating God to second place, you're dooming yourself to a second-class existence—or worse. And that's too bad, because God has better plans for you and your family.

If you want to tap into God's plan for your life, you'll need to put him right where he belongs: in first place. Putting him close to first place isn't good enough. It's just like your high-school football coach used to say: "Close only counts in horseshoes and hand grenades." Second, third, or fourth place isn't good enough for God—nor, by the way, should it be good enough for you.

Now, you may be thinking: here in the real world, putting God first is easier said than done. You're right. It isn't always easy to put obeying God ahead of everything else in your life. But it's always the right thing to do. And when you put God first, you earn lots of big rewards. One of those rewards has to do with making decisions.

When you finally make up your mind to make God the undisputed captain of your team—when you decide to put God first in every aspect of your life—decision making gets easier. Why? Because God's Word tells you what to do and, just as important, what not to do. So instead of sitting around in a state of confusion (or in the grip of temptation), you can simply get busy doing the right thing.

WE SHOULD ENCOURAGE PEOPLE IN THE GAME OF LIFE, AND WE SHOULD CHALLENGE PEOPLE TO STUDY THE WORD OF GOD.

Joe Gibbs

RECAP . . .

Putting God first means obeying him first, worshiping him first, praising him first, and serving him first. Period. If God is your captain, you're a winner. If he's not, you're not.

IN THE HUDDLE

TALK TO your friends about putting God first in every aspect of your lives, including the things you watch on TV. Talk about the messages you receive from the popular media, and compare those messages to the teachings of God's Word. Discuss ways you can protect yourselves and your families from the temptations and distractions of everyday life. And while you're at it, ask this question: does God really approve of every single TV show (and movie) my family watches?

GAME PLAN

MAKE YOUR home a TV-free zone at least one night a week. You probably watch lots of sports on TV—and lots of other stuff too. If so, you and your family members are being bombarded with images and ideas—many of which are, at best, a waste of time and, at worst, a powerful negative influence. So try this experiment: Turn off all the televisions in your house at least one night a week. Spend that evening talking with your family about life, love, and God. It's up to you as a parent to exercise thoughtful control and make sure your kids don't channel surf their way through life.

NO TEST OF A MAN'S TRUE CHARACTER IS MORE CONCLUSIVE THAN HOW HE SPENDS HIS TIME AND HIS MONEY.

Patrick Morley

GAME NOTES

An important lesson I learned this week:

_____

_____

_____

_____

_____

What I feel God is telling me this week:

_____

_____

_____

_____

_____

How I'll put this week's game plan into action:

_____

_____

_____

_____

_____

_____

_____

_____

_____

_____

_____

A WORD FROM THE COACH

Concentrate on doing your best for God,
work you won't be ashamed of, laying
out the truth plain and simple.

—2 Timothy 2:15 MSG

YOUR "A" GAME

WARMUPS

- Are you waiting for fortune to drop in your lap?

- Are you whining more and winning less, or are you determined to work your way to the top despite life's inevitable setbacks?

- Do you think winning should be easy, or are you willing to work for your victories?

GOING DEEP

FACE IT: everybody in your family likes to eat, and they'd all prefer to live indoors. That means somebody (or more than one somebody) has to bring home the bacon. And most likely one of those somebodies is the good-looking fellow you see in the mirror.

In some countries you might have to work eighty hours a week just to keep your family fed; but in America it's usually a lot easier than that. You probably won't have to work twelve-hour days to make ends meet. In the land of the free and the home of the brave, you can earn big rewards by working forty or fifty hours a week—if you're willing to work hard and smart, which means bringing your "A" game to work. Every day.

> WORK IS DOING IT.
> DISCIPLINE IS DOING IT
> EVERY DAY. DILIGENCE
> IS DOING IT WELL
> EVERY DAY.
>
> *Dave Ramsey*

Grambling State University's legendary football coach Eddie Robinson observed, "You can have anything you want if you're willing to pay the price." Well, maybe you can have almost anything you want if you're willing to work hard enough for it. But here's a little word of warning: while America is a land of opportunities, it's not a land of guarantees. If you're not willing to do the work, you shouldn't expect to reap the rewards.

Thomas Edison became one of America's most productive inventors despite the fact that his formal education was limited to a mere three months. When questioned about his success, Edison spoke these now famous words: "Genius is one percent inspiration and ninety-nine percent perspiration." Edison and his associates invented the first practical incandescent light, the phonograph, motion-picture equipment, and more than a thousand other patented devices. These impressive accomplishments came not just from creative genius but from endless hours of old-fashioned, shoulder-to-the-wheel perseverance. Edison's hard work paid off—and yours can too.

The Bible talks a lot about hard work. In his second letter to the Thessalonians, Paul warned, "If you don't work, you don't eat" (3:10 CEV). And the book of Proverbs says, "One who is slack in his work is brother to one who destroys" (18:9 NIV). In short, God has created a world in which diligence is rewarded and laziness is not. So whatever you decide to do, do it with excitement, with commitment, and with determination. And remember this: hard work is not simply a proven way to get ahead; it's also part of God's plan for you.

You'll find countless opportunities to accomplish great things for God—just don't expect the tasks to be easy. But don't shy away from them either. Pray as if everything depended on God, and work as if everything depended on you. Then, when you and God become partners, you can expect amazing things to happen.

> THERE IS NO SUBSTITUTE FOR HARD WORK AND EFFORT BEYOND THE CALL OF MERE DUTY. THAT IS WHAT STRENGTHENS THE SOUL AND ENNOBLES ONE'S CHARACTER.
>
> *Walter Camp*

RECAP . . .

Big victories require total commitment, which is OK with God. After all, he didn't create you for a life of mediocrity; he created you for greatness. Do you want to be a winner? Then expect your victories to come after you've done the work, not before.

IN THE HUDDLE

ASK THE guys how they feel about their work. See how many of your buddies are working hard and "making it happen" for their families. And while you're at it, ask yourself if you're spending the time and energy necessary to be a success in the career you've chosen. If the answer to that question is yes, keep up the good work. If the answer is no, ask yourself what it will take to make you bring your "A" game to the workplace.

GAME PLAN

RAISE THE level of your game by changing one bad habit at work. Nobody's perfect, and that includes you. There's always a little room for improvement (and for some of us, it's a bigger room than we'd like to admit). Think for a minute about where you might have room for improvement in your current job. Then ask yourself this question: if God told me that, with the snap of my finger, I could break one bad habit at work, what would it be? When you identify your single "baddest" habit, prayerfully ask God to help you fix it, starting today.

THE HIGHER THE IDEAL, THE MORE WORK IS REQUIRED TO ACCOMPLISH IT. DO NOT EXPECT TO BECOME A GREAT SUCCESS IN LIFE IF YOU ARE NOT WILLING TO WORK FOR IT.

Father Flanagan

GAME NOTES

An important lesson I learned this week:

_____

_____

_____

_____

_____

What I feel God is telling me this week:

_____

_____

_____

_____

_____

_____

How I'll put this week's game plan into action:

_____

_____

_____

_____

_____

_____

_____

_____

_____

_____

_____

_____

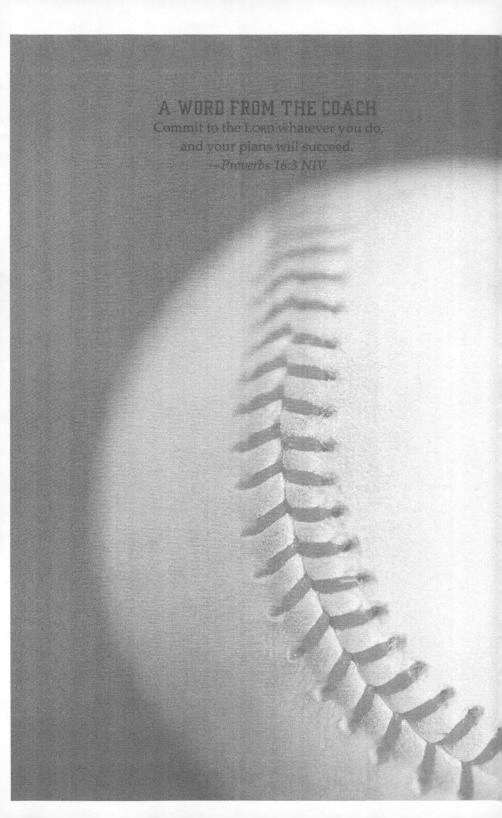

A WORD FROM THE COACH

Commit to the LORD whatever you do,
and your plans will succeed.
—*Proverbs 16:3 NIV*

PREPARING YOUR GAME PLAN

WARMUPS

- Do you have a specific, clearly defined plan for the game of life, or are you winging it?

- If you have a plan, does it line up with God's plan?

GOING DEEP

HAVE YOU got a game plan for life—a master plan that lines up with the Master's plan? Or are you bopping along the road of life without a map or a destination? If you have no idea where you want to go, any old road will take you there—but if you're like most guys, you'd probably rather have a little more control than that over the direction of your life.

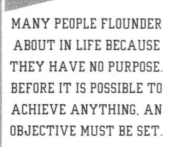

MANY PEOPLE FLOUNDER ABOUT IN LIFE BECAUSE THEY HAVE NO PURPOSE. BEFORE IT IS POSSIBLE TO ACHIEVE ANYTHING, AN OBJECTIVE MUST BE SET.

George Halas

Face facts, brother: you're much more likely to hit the mark if you're looking at the right target—and if you take time to aim. So if you want to achieve success (and the prosperity that often accompanies it), consult your Advisor and start planning now.

A clearly marked road map for life can be a powerful tool for acquiring the things you want and need. As you map out your course, here are some things to keep in mind:

- *Make your goals specific.* Fuzzy planning leads to confusion; precise planning produces results.

- *Make your goals challenging but achievable.* Realistic goals will motivate you; unrealistic goals will discourage you.

- *Write down your goals.* Paper is cheap, and your future is worth it.

- *Review your goals often.* Every day is best. If you find that you just don't have time to review your plans for the future, it's probably time to turn off the TV and review your priorities.

- *Make your goals measurable.* Don't forget that measurability means including a timetable for completion. Measure your progress at regular intervals.

- *Consider sharing your dreams with at least one supportive, encouraging person.* That person may be a spouse or parent. But if your family and friends tend to pour cold water on your dreams, feel free to make dreaming a solo sport until you find a genuine cheerleader.

- *If things change, don't be afraid to adjust your goals.* A good plan allows for midcourse corrections.

- *Be persistent.* If you give up at the first sign of trouble, you'll never achieve your goals. But if you keep plugging, even when you'd rather call it quits, you'll discover that perseverance pays.

SET YOUR GOALS UP THERE REAL HIGH, AND THEN BE SERIOUS ABOUT REACHING THEM.

Don Maynard

The Bible has lots to say about planning too, especially in the book of Proverbs. Whatever you do, make sure your plans line up with God's, because his Word tells us: "I know the plans I have for you . . . plans to prosper you and not to harm you, plans to give you hope and a future" (Jeremiah 29:11 NIV). Playing on God's team is definitely a winning strategy.

RECAP . . .

If you want to be a winner in life, you need a solid game plan. But even as you plan for the future, entrust the final outcome to God. Plan thoughtfully, work carefully, and wait patiently. Remember that God, too, is at work. And with him on your side, your ultimate victory is guaranteed.

IN THE HUDDLE

MAKE IT a point to stay in contact with guys whose life plans line up with God's will. Find out how they establish their priorities, what motivates them, and what methods they use. Ask them how they measure their progress and how they maintain their momentum. Then take the best ideas you find, and incorporate those ideas into your own.

GAME PLAN

MAKE YOUR goals SMART:

SPECIFIC: know precisely where you want to go.

MEASURABLE: be able to measure your success.

ACTION-ORIENTED: break your plan into specific steps.

REALISTIC: achievable goals provide incentive; pie-in-the-sky goals don't.

TIMELY: set deadlines, and stick to them.

NO MATTER HOW MUCH TIME YOU HAVE WASTED
IN THE PAST, YOU CAN STILL HAVE AN ENTIRE TOMORROW.
SUCCESS DEPENDS UPON USING IT WISELY—
BY PLANNING AND SETTING PRIORITIES.

Denis Waitley

GAME NOTES

An important lesson I learned this week:

_____
_____
_____
_____
_____

What I feel God is telling me this week:

_____
_____
_____
_____
_____

How I'll put this week's game plan into action:

_____
_____
_____
_____
_____
_____
_____
_____
_____
_____

A WORD FROM THE COACH

The righteous man walks in his integrity;
his children are blessed after him.

—Proverbs 20:7 NKJV

BIG SHOT ACCORDING TO WHOM?

WARMUPS

- Here's a quick quiz: whose expectations are you trying to meet?

  a. Your friends'
  b. Society's
  c. God's

  (If you answered a or b, it's time to dust off your Bible and start reading.)

GOING DEEP

DEEP DOWN, most of us guys want to be big shots. Most of us would prefer to be seen as cool, collected, and competent, not jittery, inept, or inexperienced. We'd rather play quarterback than left guard, we'd rather be a starter than a substitute, and we'd rather be the hero than the goat. It's only natural.

So if you're one of those guys who seeks the admiration of your neighbors, your coworkers, your pals, and your family, don't worry too much: you're normal. But your eagerness to please others should never overshadow your eagerness to please God. When it comes to being a big shot, you've got to keep things in perspective by trying to please God first and everybody else next. No exceptions.

> REPUTATION IS WHAT MAN SAYS ABOUT YOU; CHARACTER IS WHAT GOD KNOWS ABOUT YOU.
>
> *Bobby Bowden*

People everywhere are engaged in a colossal, worldwide treasure hunt. Some seek the treasures that come from earthly sources, such as material wealth or public acclaim; others seek godly treasures, such as character, faith, and integrity, making God the cornerstone of their lives.

What kind of treasure hunter are you? Are you so caught up in the need to impress your friends and neighbors that you sometimes allow the search for worldly stuff to become your primary focus? Are you so worried about keeping up with the Joneses that you fail to keep up with Jesus? Are you so hung up on being a big shot with the boys that you lose sight of the big job God has for you? If so, it's time to call a time-out and have a little chat with your heavenly Play Caller. When you do, God will teach you—through his Word and through the conscience he has placed within your heart—that impressing your peers is pointless if, by doing so, you fail to impress your Creator.

Would you like a proven strategy for successful living?

Here's a formula that's time tested and true: Forget about being a big shot in the eyes of your friends, your neighbors, or even your family members. Don't worry too much about impressing people with the stuff you own or the image you've created. Concern yourself, instead, with the way you appear to God. After all, God knows the real you, and he's ready to reward you when you do the right thing. So don't make him wait another day longer.

> A MAN WHO LIVES RIGHT,
> AND IS RIGHT, HAS MORE
> POWER IN HIS SILENCE
> THAN ANOTHER HAS BY
> HIS WORDS.
>
> *Phillips Brooks*

RECAP . . .

Too many guys invest too much energy trying to make themselves look like big shots in the eyes of their friends and neighbors—and too little energy trying to look good to the only one who really counts: God. Your assignment, if you choose to accept it, is to forget about being the big man on campus and start worrying about being a big man in the eyes of your Father in heaven.

IN THE HUDDLE

TALK TO your friends about how it feels to win and how it feels to lose. Then talk about winning and losing, not from your own perspective, but from God's perspective.

GAME PLAN

WANT TO be a righteous man? Hang out with righteous men. Righteousness, like so many other human characteristics, is contagious. So your job is to find the right group of guys and join it. And while you're at it, avoid people and places that might tempt you to disobey God's commandments. When you do these things, you'll improve your odds of doing the right thing today and every day.

I DON'T BELIEVE IN MIRACLES.
I BELIEVE IN CHARACTER.

Pat Dye

GAME NOTES

An important lesson I learned this week:

_____

_____

_____

_____

_____

What I feel God is telling me this week:

_____

_____

_____

_____

_____

How I'll put this week's game plan into action:

_____

_____

_____

_____

_____

_____

_____

_____

_____

_____

A WORD FROM THE COACH

He who had received five talents came and brought five other talents, saying, "Lord, you delivered to me five talents; look, I have gained five more talents besides them." His lord said to him, "Well done, good and faithful servant; you were faithful over a few things, I will make you ruler over many things. Enter into the joy of your lord."

—*Matthew 25:20–21 NKJV*

SCOUTING YOUR TALENT

WARMUPS

- God has given you a specific set of talents and opportunities. Have you clearly identified those talents, and are you working to refine them?

- How are you using your talents and opportunities to serve God?

GOING DEEP

IF YOU'RE going to be a star in the world of sports, you don't just need to have talent (lots of guys have that)—you also need to do something with that talent. In other words, you must be willing to do the hard work of turning raw ability into polished skill.

The same rule applies in life: if you want to be a winner, you must make the most of the talents God has given you.

Make no mistake, big guy, God knew precisely what he was doing when he gave you a unique set of talents and opportunities. And now your heavenly Father is waiting to see exactly what you're going to do with those gifts. So here's the big question: are you going to use those talents in the service of your Creator?

> I AM BLESSED WITH A TALENT, AND I HAVE AN OBLIGATION TO THE LORD TO MAKE THE MOST OF IT.
>
> *Andre Agassi*

God instructs all of us to be faithful stewards of the gifts he bestows on us, but the world tempts us to do otherwise. Ours is a society with countless opportunities to squander our time, our resources, and our talents. So we must be watchful for distractions and temptations that might lead us down the primrose path and away from God's path for our lives.

Every time you tee up in the game of life, you have a choice to make: nurture your talents or neglect them. When you choose wisely, God rewards your efforts and expands your opportunities to serve him.

If you're sincerely interested in building a successful life, build it using the talents God, in his infinite wisdom, has given you. Don't try to build a career around the talents you wish he'd given you. God has blessed you with unique opportunities to serve him, and he has given you every tool you need to do so.

Today accept this challenge: value the talent God has given you, nourish it, make it grow, and share it with the world. After all, the best way to say thank you for God's gifts is to use them.

> # EACH OF US HAS BEEN PUT ON EARTH WITH THE ABILITY TO DO SOMETHING WELL. WE CHEAT OURSELVES AND THE WORLD IF WE DON'T USE THAT ABILITY AS BEST WE CAN.
>
> *George Allen*

RECAP . . .

You're the proud owner of a special set of talents that can be nurtured carefully or ignored totally. The challenge, of course, is to use your abilities to the greatest extent possible. Your talents are priceless gifts from the Creator, and the way to say thank you for God's gifts is to use them.

IN THE HUDDLE

TALK WITH your friends about the talents each of you wishes you had (to be an astronaut, Internet billionaire, world's best golfer, leading man, etc.). Then talk about the talents you actually have. Discuss ways you can build upon your real strengths by focusing more intently on the abilities God has given you (not the ones he hasn't).

GAME PLAN

PAY CAREFUL attention to what the Bible says about you and your talents. Take time to consider what the parable of the talents (read Matthew 25:14–30) means to you. When you do, you'll see that God clearly instructs all of us to do the hard work of refining our talents (and taking risks) for the glory of his kingdom and the service of his people. If you do that, you'll be blessed.

YOU ARE THE ONLY PERSON ON EARTH
WHO CAN USE YOUR ABILITY.

Zig Ziglar

GAME NOTES

An important lesson I learned this week:

_____

_____

_____

_____

_____

What I feel God is telling me this week:

_____

_____

_____

_____

_____

How I'll put this week's game plan into action:

_____

_____

_____

_____

_____

_____

_____

_____

_____

_____

_____

A WORD FROM THE COACH

The thing you should want most is God's kingdom
and doing what God wants. Then all these
other things you need will be given to you.
—*Matthew 6:33 NCV*

CALLING THE PLAYS

WARMUPS

- Do you have a daily to-do list, and do you prioritize the things on that list in terms of their relative importance?

- As you're planning for the day ahead, do you include God in your plans?

GOING DEEP

NOBODY EVER said calling plays was easy. If it's a weekday, you've probably got a long to-do list at your job (not to be confused with the honey-do list your sweetheart probably gives you on weekends). And if you're as smart as I think you are, you'll have a to-do list for God's work too. So with lots of things to do and only twenty-four hours in a day, you're probably a pretty busy fellow. That means you've got to prioritize.

> IF I WERE STARTING MY FAMILY OVER AGAIN, I WOULD GIVE FIRST PRIORITY TO MY WIFE AND CHILDREN, NOT TO MY WORK.
>
> *Richard Halverson*

On your daily to-do list, all items are not created equal: certain tasks are extremely important, while others are less crucial. So it's important to prioritize your daily activities and complete each task in the approximate order of its importance.

The principle of doing first things first is simple in theory but more complicated in practice. Well-meaning family, friends, and coworkers have a way of making unexpected demands upon your time. Furthermore, each day has its own share of minor emergencies—urgent matters that tend to draw your attention away from more important ones. To act on your priorities in the real world requires maturity, patience, and determination.

If you don't prioritize your day, life will do it for you. So your choice is simple: prioritize or be prioritized. It's a choice that will largely determine the quality of your life. And what should your number one priority be? Well, that's where God comes in. If you don't put God first in your life, you're headed for trouble, and fast.

Once you've made certain that God is your first priority, the next step is to divide your daily to-do list into three levels of importance:

1. Must do

2. Ought to do (if there's time)

3. May get around to doing (if there's lots of time)

If you have trouble deciding which tasks on your list should go into which category, take a time-out and talk to the Coach. Then, when you've ranked everything according to its level of importance, do the most important stuff first—even if you'd rather be doing something else.

So here's a tip from the Swan: put your Creator where he belongs—at the very center of your day and your life—and talk to him often. When you do, the rest of your priorities will usually fall into place.

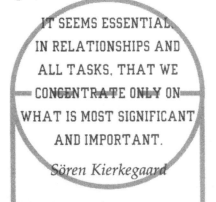

IT SEEMS ESSENTIAL IN RELATIONSHIPS AND ALL TASKS, THAT WE CONCENTRATE ONLY ON WHAT IS MOST SIGNIFICANT AND IMPORTANT.

Sören Kierkegaard

RECAP . . .

As you organize your day and your life, you'll need to decide where God fits in. Do you squeeze him in on Sundays and at mealtimes? Or do you consult him on a moment-to-moment basis about all the things on your to-do list? The answers to these questions will determine the direction of your life's journey, the quality of that journey, and its ultimate destination.

IN THE HUDDLE

HERE'S SOMETHING for you and the guys to talk over: are there enough hours in the day to take care of your most important priorities? You may not feel like there are. But God made each day just the right length. If you and your buddies are falling behind in your tasks, discuss what might be some misplaced priorities. Team up to help one another figure out how to get that to-do list in tip-top shape.

GAME PLAN

SETTING PRIORITIES may mean saying no. Face it: you can't do everything, which means you need to learn how to say no politely, firmly, and maybe more frequently. Consider today the ways you've allowed other people or circumstances to set your priorities for you, and make a new to-do list, keeping God as the center. As incentive, also list some ways you and your family will be better off when you learn to say no to the tasks you really shouldn't take on.

IF YOU'VE FOUND YOURSELF BREATHLESSLY CHASING THE GUY IN FRONT OF YOU, BREAK FREE. . . . LIFE IS SIMPLY TOO SHORT TO BE SPENT PLODDING AROUND IN ENDLESS CIRCLES.

James Dobson

GAME NOTES

An important lesson I learned this week:

_____

_____

_____

_____

_____

What I feel God is telling me this week:

_____

_____

_____

_____

_____

How I'll put this week's game plan into action:

_____

_____

_____

_____

_____

_____

_____

_____

_____

_____

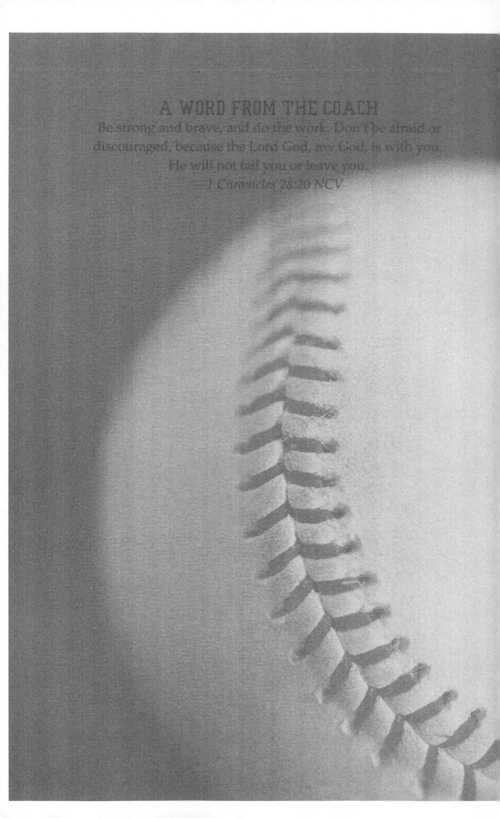

A WORD FROM THE COACH

Be strong and brave, and do the work. Don't be afraid or discouraged, because the Lord God, my God, is with you. He will not fail you or leave you.

—*1 Chronicles 28:20 NCV*

GUT CHECK

WARMUPS

- When have you fallen into the bad habit of ignoring problems or, worse yet, running from them?

- When have you found the courage to do exactly what needs to be done when it needs to be done?

GOING DEEP

IN THE world of sports, we're always talking about courage. But when it comes to good old-fashioned guts, few folks can hold a candle to the adventurers who blast off into space.

Would you have the courage to strap yourself into a tiny capsule bolted to the top of a ten-story rocket filled to the brim with enough juice to blow you from here to kingdom come and let the folks in the control room light the match?

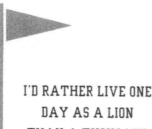

I'D RATHER LIVE ONE DAY AS A LION THAN A THOUSAND DAYS AS A LAMB.

Rick Pitino

That's exactly what the brave men and women of the astronaut corps have done for decades. One of those courageous men is Neil Armstrong, the first person to set foot on the moon.

Armstrong was born in Ohio, served his country in Korea, and became a civilian test pilot before he joined NASA as an astronaut in 1962. As commander of *Apollo 11*, he made history when he took "one small step for a man, one giant leap for mankind." When questioned later about his fears of not returning from the moon, Neil Armstrong replied: "We planned for every negative contingency, but we expected success." And that's a sound strategy for all of us.

Each of us will find his courage tested by the inevitable disappointments and tragedies of life. After all, ours is a world filled with uncertainty, hardship, sickness, and danger. Old Man Trouble, it seems, is never far from the door.

If we focus on our fears and doubts, we'll find many reasons to lie awake at night fretting about the uncertainties of the coming day. A better way is to focus not on our fears but on our God.

God is as near as your next breath, and he's in control. He offers his gift of love to all his children, including you. If you choose to accept that gift, God will be your shield and your strength, and you'll be his child forever. So don't dwell on the fears of the day. Trust God's plan and his eternal love for you. Remember, God is good, and he will have the last word.

If you'd like your life to successfully blast off, follow Armstrong's lead: plan for the worst, but expect the best. Don't ignore your fears, but don't be ruled by them either. If you'll prepare wisely and go forward confidently, you can shoot for the moon knowing that godly men of courage aren't even limited by the sky!

YOU'LL NEVER REACH SECOND BASE IF YOU KEEP ONE FOOT ON FIRST.

Vernon Law

RECAP . . .

You can have the courage to do what you need to do when you remember that God is the source of your strength. He isn't on vacation, and he hasn't clocked out for lunch. He's right here, right now, ready to help his children—and that means you. Call on him in your hour of need, and take heart. Whatever the size of your challenge, God is bigger.

IN THE HUDDLE

DON'T BE afraid to discuss your fears and apprehensions with close friends and family members. As you talk things over with your pals, you'll be reminded that facing fear is a far better strategy than running from it. And you'll find ways to give each other courage along the way.

GAME PLAN

INCREASE YOUR supply of courage by sharing it. Courage is contagious. When it's inspired by steadfast trust in a loving heavenly Father, it's highly contagious. Today, as you interact with friends, family members, or coworkers, share your courage, your hopes, your dreams, and your enthusiasm. Your positive outlook will be almost as big a blessing to them as it is to you.

NEVER FLINCH; NEVER WEARY; NEVER DESPAIR.

Winston Churchill

GAME NOTES

An important lesson I learned this week:

_____

_____

_____

_____

_____

What I feel God is telling me this week:

_____

_____

_____

_____

_____

How I'll put this week's game plan into action:

_____

_____

_____

_____

_____

_____

_____

_____

_____

_____

_____

_____

_____

A WORD FROM THE COACH

The peace of God, which surpasses every thought, will guard your hearts and your minds in Christ Jesus. Finally brothers, whatever is true, whatever is honorable, whatever is just, whatever is pure, whatever is lovely, whatever is commendable—if there is any moral excellence and if there is any praise—dwell on these things.

—Philippians 4:7–8 HCSB

YOUR MENTAL GAME

WARMUPS

- Are you constantly trying to improve your mental game by taking control of the tone and direction of your thoughts?

- Or are you an undisciplined thinker who is regularly carried away by irrational thoughts and unchecked emotions?

GOING DEEP

ARE YOU the master of your thoughts or a slave to them? Hopefully, you've learned how to keep your thoughts within the boundaries God has set. Otherwise, you may be headed for trouble.

Our thoughts have the power to lift us up or drag us down; they can energize or deplete us, inspire us to greater accomplishments or make those feats impossible. When we learn to keep our thoughts on the right track—when we honor God with our meditations and deliberations—we will be blessed. But if we allow our thoughts to run off like a bunch of wild squirrels, we'll be shakier than Barney Fife at a bank robbers' convention.

> PEOPLE WHO DO NOT DEVELOP AND PRACTICE GOOD THINKING OFTEN FIND THEMSELVES AT THE MERCY OF THEIR CIRCUMSTANCES.
>
> *John Maxwell*

Perhaps you're upbeat, a man whose hopes and dreams are alive and well. You keep a smile on your face and a song in your heart. But everyone faces times when pessimism, anger, or doubt threaten to throw his emotions off course. When that happens to you, you won't feel much like rejoicing. That's why it's important to push past your pain and focus on thinking rightly if you're going to make it successfully to the finish line.

God wants you to experience joy and abundance, but he won't force it on you. Today and every day, it's up to you to celebrate the life God has given you by keeping your head in the game—focusing on things that are excellent and worthy of praise.

IF OUR MINDS ARE STAYED
UPON GOD, HIS PEACE
WILL RULE THE AFFAIRS
ENTERTAINED BY OUR
MINDS. IF, ON THE OTHER
HAND, WE ALLOW OUR
MINDS TO DWELL ON THE
CARES OF THIS WORLD, GOD'S
PEACE WILL BE FAR FROM
OUR THOUGHTS.

Woodroll Kroll

RECAP . . .

Our thoughts have power to affect our lives—for better or worse. Focusing too intently on things that distance us from God can lead to great harm. But right thoughts can help lift our spirits, improve our circumstances, and strengthen our relationship with the Creator.

IN THE HUDDLE

HERE'S AN experiment for you and your buddies: Instead of watching late-night television, turn off the TV and read the Bible. Or read uplifting literature. Or listen to inspirational music. If you fill your mind with good thoughts each night, you'll probably find yourself sleeping better and enjoying a more optimistic outlook when you wake up the next morning.

GAME PLAN

SHUT DOWN the complaint department—for good! Do you ever find yourself having a pity party? If so, it's time to start spending more time thinking about your blessings and less time fretting about your hardships. Then, when you've come to your senses, it's time to say a great big word of thanks to your Father in heaven. After all, he's already given you more gifts than you can possibly count.

THINK ALL OF THE TIME. STUDY YOUR OPPONENT AND YOURSELF ALL OF THE TIME FOR THE PURPOSE OF INCREASING YOUR EFFECTIVENESS AND DIMINISHING HIS.

John Wooden

GAME NOTES

An important lesson I learned this week:

_____

_____

_____

_____

_____

What I feel God is telling me this week:

_____

_____

_____

_____

_____

_____

How I'll put this week's game plan into action:

_____

_____

_____

_____

_____

_____

_____

_____

_____

_____

_____

_____

A WORD FROM THE COACH

Love must be without hypocrisy. Detest evil; cling to what
is good. Show family affection to one another with
brotherly love. Outdo one another in showing honor.
—*Romans 12:9–10 HCSB*

TAKING CARE OF THE HOME TEAM

WARMUPS

- Are you willing to put God first, your family second, and everything else third?

- Do you ever let other things—things like work, sports, entertainment, or hobbies—take priority over family matters?

GOING DEEP

HOW DO you treat your home team? Are you one of those guys who lives by the creed "God first and family second"? Or do you put other things ahead of your Creator and your clan? If you're a God-and-family kind of guy, congratulations! You're doing God's work by obeying his Word. But if you've mistakenly placed God and family somewhere behind NASCAR and football, your heavenly Father might want to have a little chat with you.

> THE FIRST AND MOST IMPORTANT TEAM IN ANYONE'S LIFE IS THEIR FAMILY.
>
> *Pat Riley*

When God gave you a family, he also gave you the responsibility of caring for that family. Period. Of course, taking care of your wife and kids isn't easy. Sometimes family life holds moments of frustration and disappointment, even for the most dedicated of men. But if you're lucky enough to live among a close-knit, caring family, you'll agree that the rewards far outweigh the demands.

Still, the reality is that we live in a competitive world, a place where earning a living can be difficult and demanding. As pressures build, we may tend to focus so intently on our financial concerns that we lose sight—at least for a while—of our other, more important responsibilities. (That's one reason a regular daily devotional time is so important: it offers a dose of perspective.)

God intends that we honor him by honoring our families. We honor our families by giving them our love, our support, our advice, our cooperation, and, when needed, some discipline. And make no mistake: these matters require significant investments of time. But it's time well spent. Former president Jimmy Carter observed, "Many of the most highly publicized events of my presidency are not nearly as memorable or significant in my life as fishing with my daddy."

Those of us who, like Mr. Carter, possess happy memories of parents and grandparents owe a profound debt to those who have gone before us. We repay that debt not to our forefathers but to our children. May God give us the strength to repay it in full.

No family is perfect, yours included. But despite the inevitable challenges of providing for your loved ones, and despite the occasional hurt feelings that come with family life, your family is God's gift to you. Give thanks to him for that gift . . . and act toward your family members in ways that show your love and thankfulness.

> YOU HAVE HEARD ABOUT "QUALITY TIME" AND "QUANTITY TIME." YOUR FAMILY NEEDS BOTH.
>
> *Jim Gallery*

RECAP . . .

Your most valuable earthly treasure is not your home, your car, or your savings account. Your most valuable earthly treasure is your family. Family is a priceless gift from God. Cherish it, protect it, and dedicate it to him. When you place God at the center of your life and your family, he will bless you and yours.

IN THE HUDDLE

TALK TO the guys about family time. Find out what they do to strengthen their family ties. Discuss ways to spend quality *and* quantity time. But don't spend too long talking—you need to get home to your families.

GAME PLAN

HAVING TROUBLE expressing your emotions? Practice, practice, practice. Since you love your family, it's only fair that you tell them so, and tell them often. Today think about ways you can let your family members know you love them. And as you're expressing your affection, make sure your actions match up with your words.

MY PRIMARY ROLE IS NOT TO BE THE BOSS AND JUST LOOK GOOD, BUT TO BE A SERVANT LEADER WHO ENABLES AND ENHANCES MY FAMILY TO BE THEIR BEST.

Tim Hansel

GAME NOTES

An important lesson I learned this week:

_____

_____

_____

_____

_____

What I feel God is telling me this week:

_____

_____

_____

_____

_____

_____

How I'll put this week's game plan into action:

_____

_____

_____

_____

_____

_____

_____

_____

_____

_____

_____

A WORD FROM THE COACH
For the happy heart, life is a continual feast.
—*Proverbs 15:15 NLT*

HOW TO PLAY HAPPY

WARMUPS

- Do you look for the silver lining in every cloud?

- Do you expect happiness to fall into your lap like manna from heaven?

- Are you willing to search for happiness even when it's hard to find?

GOING DEEP

THE GREAT center fielder Willie Mays had simple advice for ballplayers of every era. He said, "Play happy." And Willie's words of wisdom apply to you, even if you don't know the difference between a pop fly and a fruit fly. The game of life is a game that's best played by happy players.

> SUCCESS IS BEING TRULY HAPPY AT WHAT YOU DO.
>
> *Tommy Lasorda*

As people have become increasingly prosperous, the pursuit of happiness has become one of our great pastimes. We invest enormous amounts of time and energy in an almost endless variety of activities designed to make us happy. Lasting happiness, however, is not a commodity that can be "found"; it is an internal condition that results from the right kind of thoughts and the right kind of behaviors.

The pursuit of happiness is something of a paradox: often the more we rush after happiness, the more difficult it is to obtain. But if we put matters of personal happiness aside and, instead, throw ourselves into some other worthy pursuit, we find that happiness is frequently the by-product. Yet even if we're intensely working toward a worthy goal, happiness isn't guaranteed. Since true happiness comes from God, to achieve it, we must learn to play by God's rules.

Well-known author and Bible teacher Warren Wiersbe once observed, "Happiness is the by-product of a life that is lived in the will of God. When we humbly serve others, walk in God's path of holiness, and do what he tells us, then we will enjoy happiness."

Do you seek happiness, abundance, and contentment? Would you like to attain these things now, not later? If so, here's a time-tested formula: love God and his Son; depend on God for strength; try, to the best of your ability, to follow God's will; and strive to obey his Word. When you do these things, you'll discover that righteousness and happiness go hand in hand.

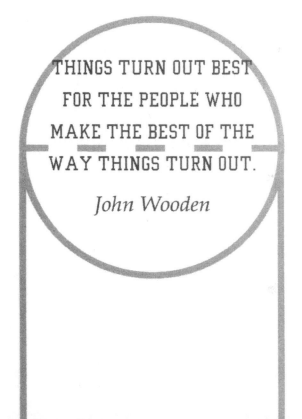

THINGS TURN OUT BEST
FOR THE PEOPLE WHO
MAKE THE BEST OF THE
WAY THINGS TURN OUT.

John Wooden

RECAP . . .

What should you expect from the coming day? A world full of possibilities (but it's up to you to seize them) and God's promise of abundance (but it's up to you to accept it). So as you prepare for the next step in your life's journey, remember this: obedience to God doesn't ensure instant happiness, but disobedience to God always makes lasting happiness impossible.

IN THE HUDDLE

TALK TO your friends about happiness—the things that cause it and the things that prevent it. Ask your buddies if they believe happiness is something you can "catch" or something that you must earn.

GAME PLAN

DON'T EXPECT uninterrupted happiness. Even if you're a fortunate guy, you shouldn't expect to be happy all the time. Sometimes things will happen that are bound to make you miserable. That's life! During those difficult days, focus your thoughts and lean on God. When you do, you'll soon discover that you're experiencing more good days than bad ones, and more happy thoughts than sad ones.

HAPPINESS DOESN'T DEPEND UPON WHO YOU ARE OR WHAT YOU HAVE; IT DEPENDS UPON WHAT YOU THINK.

Dale Carnegie

GAME NOTES

An important lesson I learned this week:

_____

_____

_____

_____

_____

What I feel God is telling me this week:

_____

_____

_____

_____

_____

How I'll put this week's game plan into action:

_____

_____

_____

_____

_____

_____

_____

_____

_____

_____

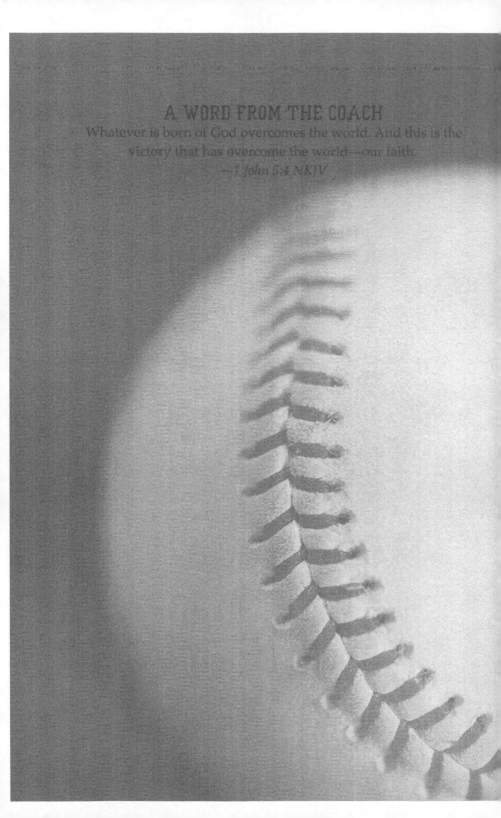

A WORD FROM THE COACH

Whatever is born of God overcomes the world. And this is the
victory that has overcome the world—our faith.

—1 John 5:4 NKJV

WHEN THE GOING GETS TOUGH

WARMUPS

- Has the great dump truck of life ever backed up to your front door and unloaded a king-sized mess in the middle of your front yard?

- Have you made the solemn promise to find ways to turn those messes into blessings?

GOING DEEP

IT'S ONE of the most familiar adages in sports: "When the going gets tough, the tough get going." And I guarantee that sometimes the going will get tough. If you participate in the game of life, you're going to get your clock cleaned from time to time, and you won't be alone.

Old Man Trouble pays occasional visits to everyone— nobody, not even the most righteous fellow on the block, is exempt. But when troubles arise, God remains faithful. And you can be certain of this: whatever "it" is, God can handle it.

YOU CAN LEARN LITTLE FROM VICTORY. YOU CAN LEARN EVERYTHING FROM DEFEAT.

Christy Mathewson

While the road of life is no easy street, that's no reason to abandon hope. Even during our darkest moments we're protected by a loving heavenly Father. And that, dear friend, is the only kind of protection that really matters.

When you're worried, God can reassure you; when you're sad, God can comfort you. When your heart is heavy, God is not just near, he is here—you need only lift your thoughts and prayers to him. When you do, he will answer. Why? Because he is the Good Shepherd, and he has promised to protect you, his sheep, now and forever. The same God who created the universe stands ready and willing to comfort you and restore your strength. And in his own time and according to his master plan, he will heal you if you invite him into your heart.

The great Bear Bryant correctly observed, "You never know how a horse will pull until you hook him to a heavy load." Have you been challenged to pull a heavy load? If so, you'll certainly need all the help you can get. Friends and family members can help carry your burden. But your greatest help will come from an unseen hand, the hand of God. It's a hand that's always outstretched . . . all you must do is reach out and take it.

REMEMBER: THERE IS ALWAYS THE POSSIBILITY THAT SOME GOOD WILL ARISE FROM AN UNFORTUNATE SITUATION.

Arthur Ashe

RECAP . . .

Life is a patchwork of good days and bad days, with better days outnumbering the tough ones. During the good days, we're tempted to take our blessings for granted (a temptation we should resist with all our might). But during life's difficult days, we discover precisely what we're made of. More important, we discover what our faith is made of. When your faith is put to the test, rest assured that God is perfectly willing—and always ready—to give you all the strength you need.

IN THE HUDDLE

MOST OF us guys are remarkably good at Monday-morning quarterbacking. We're good at looking back and analyzing how things turned out—and how things should have turned out. But if we spend too much time looking in the rearview mirror, we may run ourselves off the road of life. Talk to your friends about the tough times that continue to bother you and about ways you can learn to accept the disappointments of the past so you can be more fully involved in the present.

GAME PLAN

TALK ABOUT your tough times. If you're facing big-time adversity, don't hit the panic button—and don't keep everything bottled up inside. Instead of going underground, talk things over with your wife, with your buddies, with your pastor, and if necessary, with a trained counselor. When it comes to navigating the stormy seas of life, second, third, fourth, or even fifth opinions can be helpful.

DIFFICULTIES IN LIFE ARE INTENDED TO MAKE US BETTER, NOT BITTER.

Dan Reeves

GAME NOTES

An important lesson I learned this week:

_____

_____

_____

_____

_____

What I feel God is telling me this week:

_____

_____

_____

_____

_____

How I'll put this week's game plan into action:

_____

_____

_____

_____

_____

_____

_____

_____

_____

_____

_____

A WORD FROM THE COACH

Live full lives, full in the fullness of God. God can do anything, you know—far more than you could ever imagine or guess or request in your wildest dreams! He does it not by pushing us around but by working within us, his Spirit deeply and gently within us.

—*Ephesians 3:19–20 MSG*

BECOMING A PLAYMAKER

WARMUPS

- Would you like to become a real playmaker on the field of life? If so, you'll need to find work that you love.

- Are you willing to keep searching for that work until you find it?

GOING DEEP

OK, GUYS, here's a pop quiz about your career:

- At your workplace, are you a playmaker or a sleepwalker?

- Do you love to go to work on Monday morning, or would you rather have a tooth pulled than show up at the job site?

- Have you discovered work that excites you, or are you stuck in a job you don't really enjoy?

- Have you found something that makes you want to hop out of bed in the moring and get to work?

- And does that something make the world—and your world—a better place?

Life's too short to be stuck in a job you hate. That's why it's important to search for work that's a right fit for you. If you haven't yet discovered work that blesses you and your world, don't be discouraged. Just keep searching and keep trusting that, with God's help, you can—and will—find a meaningful way to serve your neighbors and your Creator.

> **GOOD THINGS HAPPEN TO THOSE WHO HUSTLE.**
>
> *Chuck Noll*

But even when we find ourselves laboring in jobs we don't enjoy, we can become lackadaisical about our responsibilities. But God expects us to work diligently and enthusiastically for the things we need (read 2 Thessalonians 3:10 and Colossians 3:23). He has created a world in which hard work is rewarded—and sloppy work isn't. Yet sometimes we may seek ease over excellence. We may be tempted to take shortcuts when God wants us to walk the straight and narrow.

Are you willing to work diligently for yourself, for your family, and for your God? And are you willing to engage in work that's pleasing to your Creator? If so, you can expect your heavenly Father to bring a rich harvest.

And if you have concerns about any aspect of your professional life, take those concerns to God in prayer. He will guide your steps, steady your hand, calm your fears, and reward your efforts.

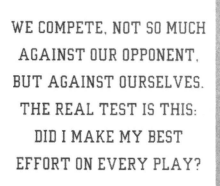

WE COMPETE. NOT SO MUCH
AGAINST OUR OPPONENT.
BUT AGAINST OURSELVES.
THE REAL TEST IS THIS:
DID I MAKE MY BEST
EFFORT ON EVERY PLAY?

Bud Wilkinson

RECAP . . .

If you've found a job you love, give thanks to God. If you haven't yet found a job you work passionately at, ask God to lead you toward a profession that pleases both you and him.

IN THE HUDDLE

TALK TO friends who are working in careers that they absolutely love. Ask them about their career paths. Then talk about ways you can discover a life's work that you love—a career that allows you to be a solid playmaker.

GAME PLAN

DARE TO *dream big . . . and often.* Your attitude toward the future will help create your future. When you think optimistically, you'll help fashion a better tomorrow (it's called the self-fulfilling prophecy). So today take a few minutes to think realistically about yourself and your current situation. Then think about your bright future, and focus on your hopes, not your fears. Ask God to help you set goals that will fit into his winning game plan for your life.

WITH THE RIGHT ATTITUDE AND A WILLINGNESS TO PAY THE PRICE, ALMOST ANYONE CAN PURSUE NEARLY ANY OPPORTUNITY AND ACHIEVE IT.

John Maxwell

GAME NOTES

An important lesson I learned this week:

_____

_____

_____

_____

_____

What I feel God is telling me this week:

_____

_____

_____

_____

_____

How I'll put this week's game plan into action:

_____

_____

_____

_____

_____

_____

_____

_____

_____

_____

A WORD FROM THE COACH

Are you tired? Worn out? Burned out on religion? Come to
me. Get away with me and you'll recover your life. I'll show
you how to take a real rest. Walk with me and work with
me—watch how I do it. Learn the unforced rhythms of grace. I
won't lay anything heavy or ill-fitting on you. Keep company
with me and you'll learn to live freely and lightly.
—*Matthew 11:28–30 MSG*

devotional 13

BED CHECK

WARMUPS

- Hey, playmaker . . . is it time to step down off the treadmill and take a breather?

- Are there changes you could make in the structure of your life that would allow you to be a little less stressed and a little more rested?

GOING DEEP

IF YOU'RE playing an away game and staying in a hotel, you'd better hit the hay when your coach tells you to. And you can expect the coach to run a bed check to be sure you and your teammates are safely in the sack (not getting yourselves into trouble). If you're supposed to be in bed at ten o'clock, you'd better be there, or else.

But what about when you're not under some coach's thumb? After all, you're a grown man, and you can stay up as late as you want, right? Well, you can burn the candle at both ends if you want, but you'll be better off if you give yourself a bed check every night to make sure you're getting enough rest.

Even the most energetic people can, from time to time, find themselves running on empty—and you're no exception. The demands of daily life can drain your strength and rob you of the joy that is yours in Christ. When you find yourself tired, discouraged, or worse, it's time to slow down and start recharging those spiritual batteries.

> WORK IS NOT ALWAYS REQUIRED OF A MAN. THERE IS SUCH A THING AS SACRED IDLENESS, THE CULTIVATION OF WHICH IS NOW FEARFULLY NEGLECTED.
>
> *George MacDonald*

God wants all of his children (including you) to lead joyous lives filled with abundance and peace. But sometimes abundance and peace can seem far away, especially when you're running on less than six hours of sleep. We live in a world that tempts us to stay up late. But too little sleep is a prescription for trouble.

Physical exhaustion is God's way of telling us to slow down. He expects us to work hard, but he also intends for us to rest. When we fail to take the rest we need, we do a big disservice to ourselves and our families.

Are your physical or spiritual batteries running low? Is your energy level flatter than a pancake? Are you too tired to care?

If so, it's time to turn your thoughts and prayers to God. And when you're finished, it's probably time to turn off the lights and go to bed.

PRESCRIPTION FOR A HAPPIER AND HEALTHIER LIFE: RESOLVE TO SLOW DOWN YOUR PACE; LEARN TO SAY NO GRACEFULLY; RESIST THE TEMPTATION TO CHASE AFTER MORE PLEASURE, MORE HOBBIES, AND MORE SOCIAL ENTANGLEMENTS.

James Dobson

RECAP . . .

For busy people living in a fast-paced, twenty-first-century world, life can seem like a merry-go-round that never stops. If that description seems to fit your life, you may find yourself running short on patience or strength or both. If you're feeling tired or discouraged, there is a source from which you can draw the power needed to renew your spirit and your strength. That source is God. Ask him to renew your strength—and realize that it's time to slow down and rest up.

IN THE HUDDLE

TALK TO your friends about how much rest they actually get—and how much rest they think they should get. Then consider your own sleeping patterns, and discuss how each of you might improve your life by improving the quality and increasing the quantity of your sleep.

GAME PLAN

TAKE THE Sabbath seriously. Working seven days a week may impress your boss, but it isn't the way God intends for you to live your life. The world doesn't often honor the Sabbath, but God wants you to treat it as a day of rest. No exceptions. So next Sunday do yourself and your family a favor: follow God's command by making the Sabbath a special day for you and your family to rest and worship him.

SATAN DOES SOME OF HIS WORST WORK ON EXHAUSTED CHRISTIANS WHEN NERVES ARE FRAYED AND THEIR MINDS ARE FAINT.

Vance Havner

GAME NOTES

An important lesson I learned this week:

_____

_____

_____

_____

_____

What I feel God is telling me this week:

_____

_____

_____

_____

_____

How I'll put this week's game plan into action:

_____

_____

_____

_____

_____

_____

_____

_____

_____

_____

_____

_____

A WORD FROM THE COACH

Now abide faith, hope, love, these three;
but the greatest of these is love.

—*1 Corinthians 13:13 NKJV*

WINNING THE GAME OF LOVE

WARMUPS

- Are you one of those guys who has trouble saying "I love you"?

- Do you find it easy to talk about NASCAR and the NFL but hard to talk about your feelings?

- Do you think it's time to start telling your loved ones that you really love them?

GOING DEEP

WINNING THE game of love is important. But talking about love isn't easy for many men. Spouting off about our emotions just doesn't seem like a manly thing to do. In fact, many of us figure we aren't even supposed to talk much about love (or any emotion even close to it). We guys think we're supposed to talk about stuff like cars (or better yet, trucks), sports, politics, yard work, and money . . . but love? No way—after all, what tough-as-nails guy wants to sound like some sort of misty-eyed Romeo?

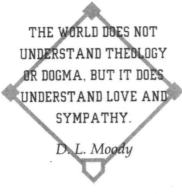

THE WORLD DOES NOT UNDERSTAND THEOLOGY OR DOGMA, BUT IT DOES UNDERSTAND LOVE AND SYMPATHY.

D. L. Moody

Too many well-meaning fellows, when questioned about matters of the heart, shrug their shoulders and ask, "What's all the fuss about?" But in the interest of writing a good devotional guide, the Swan's going to talk a little about love, and I hope you'll read it.

How do you define *love*? Is it a warm feeling you get in the pit of your stomach when you stand over the backyard grill and gaze longingly at a big, juicy slab of meat? Is it the emotion you feel when you hear there's a clearance sale at the hardware store? Or is it more than that? Hopefully, you answered, "Something more."

Among other things, love is a choice. Either you choose to behave lovingly toward other people or you don't. Either you behave in ways that enhance your relationships or you don't. There's no way around it: genuine love requires effort. If you want to build lasting relationships, you must be willing to do your part.

God allows his children to make choices for themselves, and as you interact with your family and friends, you have choices to make. If you choose wisely, you'll be rewarded; if you choose unwisely, you'll bear the consequences.

If you're a married man, you owe it to yourself, to your

wife, and to your family to express and demonstrate your love. And remember: feelings of love come and go, but genuine love chooses to hang around for the long haul. Real love is patient, understanding, consistent, and considerate. It doesn't just sit around and do nothing; it gets translated into acts of kindness, both large and small. Want to increase your odds of having a winning marriage? Tell your wife you love her—many times, every day. And make sure your behavior is an accurate reflection of your words.

But this is about the whole team too. So be sure you treat everyone in your family with respect, courtesy, and (above all) love. When you do, you'll discover that God's love is highly contagious: you catch it from the people you give it to. Loving others puts everyone in a win-win situation.

> THE BEST USE OF LIFE IS LOVE. THE BEST EXPRESSION OF LOVE IS TIME. THE BEST TIME TO LOVE IS NOW.
>
> *Rick Warren*

RECAP . . .

God wants more for you than mediocre relationships; he created you for relationships filled with his love. But building loving relationships takes compassion, wisdom, empathy, kindness, and forgiveness (lots of forgiveness). If that sounds like work, it is. But God knows you're capable of doing that work, and he knows that the fruits of your labors will enrich the lives of everyone around you.

IN THE HUDDLE

TALK TO your friends about the ways guys typically express feelings of love. Then brainstorm ways you can better express your feelings to your wives and your families.

GAME PLAN

MAKE 1 Corinthians 13 a regular part of your reading schedule. If you're a married man, read this chapter to your wife every day for a solid week. Talk about ways both of you can use this passage to enrich your marriage.

TRUE LOVE IS SPELLED G-I-V-E.
IT IS NOT BASED ON WHAT YOU CAN GET, BUT ROOTED IN
WHAT YOU CAN GIVE TO THE OTHER PERSON.

Josh McDowell

GAME NOTES

An important lesson I learned this week:

_____

_____

_____

_____

_____

What I feel God is telling me this week:

_____

_____

_____

_____

_____

_____

How I'll put this week's game plan into action:

_____

_____

_____

_____

_____

_____

_____

_____

_____

_____

_____

_____

_____

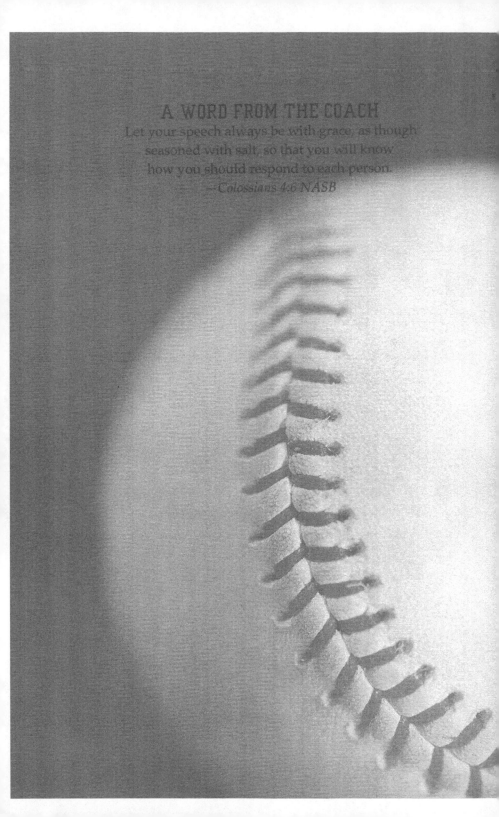

A WORD FROM THE COACH

Let your speech always be with grace, as though
seasoned with salt, so that you will know
how you should respond to each person.
—*Colossians 4:6 NASB*

TECHNICAL FOUL

WARMUPS

- Can you disagree with someone without being disagreeable, or are you the not-so-proud owner of a short fuse?

- As you look back on your past knock-down-drag-out arguments, do you wish you'd been a little less combative?

GOING DEEP

HAVE YOU ever been guilty of committing a technical foul, whether at work or at home, by spouting off first and engaging your brain later? If not, feel free to skip this chapter and move on to the next. But if you're like most guys, you've said things in anger that you wish you hadn't.

We live in a talk-show world where arguments are as plentiful as dandelion seeds on a windy spring day. But just because everybody else seems to be arguing doesn't mean you need to join the chorus. A far better strategy is to learn when to offer constructive criticism and when to keep your trap shut.

> YOU DON'T HAVE TO ATTEND EVERY ARGUMENT YOU'RE INVITED TO.
>
> *Old Saying*

Arguments, like criticism, come in at least two varieties: constructive and destructive. Debates can have positive outcomes, especially when they're conducted by mature adults who are earnestly seeking the truth. Unfortunately, most arguments don't fit that description.

The next time you feel tempted to give someone a piece of your mind, ask yourself which piece you're offering. Is it a piece of your insight or your anger? If the former, feel free to speak up and—with gentleness—share your enlightenment with the world. But if the latter, take a breath before you vent. Angry words, once spoken, can't be retrieved. It's better to think long and hard before you rant and rave.

The words you speak are more important than you may realize. They echo beyond the here and now. That's why you should seek to be an encouragement and enlightenment to others, not a constant critic or an angry adversary.

So avoid anguished outpourings. Suppress your impulsive outbursts. Curb the need to criticize. Terminate tantrums. Learn to speak words that lift others up as you share a message of help and hope to a world that needs both.

When you talk, choose language you would use if God were listening to your every word. Because he is.

SOME FIGHTS ARE LOST
EVEN THOUGH WE WIN.
A BULLDOG CAN WHIP A
SKUNK, BUT IT JUST ISN'T
WORTH IT.

Vance Havner

RECAP . . .

When you win an argument, what have you really gained? Usually, not much. So think twice before you allow yourself to get dragged into a disagreement over something that's not worth disagreeing about. And even if it is, choose with care how you communicate your point of view.

IN THE HUDDLE

TALK TO your buddies about the nature of arguments—which are productive and which are futile. Discuss ways you can redirect a conversation to avoid or extricate yourself from an argument. Then, next time you feel the urge to engage in verbal combat, ask yourself if the exchange will be worth the time and energy—and whether it will help the other person. If not, walk away.

GAME PLAN

WRITE A scouting report for your tantrums. If you'd like to defeat temper tantrums before they start—which, by the way, is the best time to beat them—try writing down a detailed "scouting report" of the people and situations that set you off. Then write down better, more productive ways to deal with these encounters. The best time to tackle trouble is before it gets rolling, not after.

DIVISIONS BETWEEN CHRISTIANS ARE A SIN AND A SCANDAL.
AND CHRISTIANS OUGHT AT ALL TIMES TO BE MAKING
CONTRIBUTIONS TOWARD REUNION,
IF IT IS ONLY BY THEIR PRAYERS.

C. S. Lewis

GAME NOTES

An important lesson I learned this week:

_____
_____
_____
_____
_____

What I feel God is telling me this week:

_____
_____
_____
_____
_____
_____

How I'll put this week's game plan into action:

_____
_____
_____
_____
_____
_____
_____
_____
_____
_____
_____
_____
_____

A WORD FROM THE COACH

Let us run the race that is before us and never give up.
We should remove from our lives anything that would
get in the way and the sin that so easily holds us back.

—*Hebrews 12:1 NCV*

LEARNING TO PICK YOUR SPOTS

WARMUPS

- Take a look at the landscape of your life. Are you overstressed because you're overcommitted?

- When somebody wants you to add yet another obligation to your already-stretched-thin schedule, do you say yes even when your conscience tells you to say no?

- Would the quality of your life be better if you cut back on your obligations so you could do fewer things, but do them better?

GOING DEEP

ADMIT IT: you like being the playmaker—the guy who comes to the rescue, the guy who fixes what's broken, the guy who gets things done. And, of course, getting things done is good . . . but you've got to learn to pick your spots.

If you're playing within your limits and not trying to stretch yourself too thin, keep up the good work. But if you're trying to do too much, if you're trying to be everything and do everything for everybody, you might burn out faster than a match in a wind tunnel.

When you allow yourself to take on too many jobs, you simply can't do all of them well. That means if you allow yourself to become overcommitted, whether at home, at work, at church, or anywhere in between, you're asking for trouble. So you must learn how to say no to the things you don't have the time or energy to do.

> SHOW ME A GUY WHO CAN'T SAY NO, AND I'LL SHOW YOU A GUY WITH LOTS OF PROBLEMS.
>
> *Red Auerbach*

But I know what you're thinking: sometimes saying no can be tough. Why? Because well-meaning guys (like you) genuinely want to help other people. But if you allow your cart to become overloaded, pretty soon you'll start underserving—and you'll disappoint just about everybody, including yourself.

Guys who overcommit and underserve lead lives filled with frequent foul-ups and endless complications. They find themselves feeling overworked, underappreciated, overstressed, and underpaid. So simplify your life by pledging to take on only those things that you can do—and do well. And while you're at it, treat your time as you would treat any other priceless asset. When you do, you'll soon be amazed at the changes a simple two-letter word—a word that begins with *n* and ends with *o*—can make in your life.

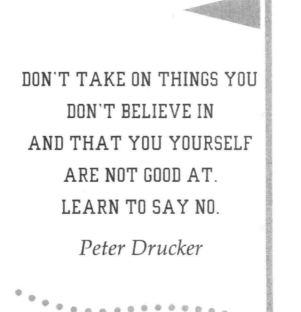

DON'T TAKE ON THINGS YOU
DON'T BELIEVE IN
AND THAT YOU YOURSELF
ARE NOT GOOD AT.
LEARN TO SAY NO.

Peter Drucker

RECAP . . .

You can either do lots of things fairly well (or maybe a little worse than that), or you can do a few things really well. If you're wise, you'll decide how many things you're willing to do well, and you'll say no to just about everything else.

IN THE HUDDLE

TALK TO your buddies about the drawbacks of being overcommitted. Discuss whether it's better to do a few jobs well or many jobs not so well. And talk about the wisdom of saying no to things you simply cannot or should not do.

GAME PLAN

CHECK TO be sure the game plan for your week isn't weak. Jot down all the activities that vie for your time in a typical week, including obligations at home, at work, at church, and in your community. As you look at that list, ask yourself if you really have time to do all those jobs well. If the answer is yes, change nothing. If not, pick at least one activity to cut out of your schedule. And keep cutting until you're no longer overcommitted.

DON'T JUST GRAB AT THE FIRST THING THAT COMES ALONG. KNOW WHEN TO REFUSE SOMETHING THAT WON'T GO ANYWHERE.

Will Rogers

GAME NOTES

An important lesson I learned this week:

_____

_____

_____

_____

_____

What I feel God is telling me this week:

_____

_____

_____

_____

_____

How I'll put this week's game plan into action:

_____

_____

_____

_____

_____

_____

_____

_____

_____

_____

_____

A WORD FROM THE COACH

Good-tempered leaders invigorate lives;
they're like spring rain and sunshine.
—*Proverbs 16:15 MSG*

HANDLING THE HEAT

WARMUPS

- Do you view yourself as a leader, whether at work, home, or church?

- Are you pleased with the quality of leadership you're providing?

- Are you the kind of leader you would want to follow?

GOING DEEP

SOMEWHERE BACK in the deep, dark recesses of your memory, as you think back upon the glory days of your sporting career, you may remember a time when your coach gave a locker-room speech that contained the quote, "If you can't stand the heat, get out of the kitchen." Well, the coach wasn't quoting Vince Lombardi or John Wooden; those words were uttered by good ol' Harry Truman, the plainspoken American president who learned about life's hot kitchens from hard experience.

> LEADERSHIP IS THE KNACK OF GETTING SOMEBODY TO DO SOMETHING YOU WANT DONE BECAUSE HE WANTS TO DO IT.
>
> *Dwight D. Eisenhower*

As commander in chief during the final days of World War II, the feisty Mr. Truman faced many tough decisions, and he never dodged them. Instead, he followed the advice of another president, Andrew Jackson, who once said, "Take time to deliberate; but when the time for action arrives, stop thinking and go in."

If Truman were here today, he'd probably be quick to point out that genuine leadership is not a popularity contest. Far from it. Genuine leadership often requires tough decisions—and decisions, by their very nature, are displeasing to some. But effective leaders are willing to sacrifice popularity for results.

Whenever you find yourself in a position of leadership—whether at church, home, work, or school—it's up to you to set the right tone by making good decisions and by setting a proper example. But keep in mind that wise leaders don't take things too seriously. The best leaders know how to laugh (when it's appropriate), when to have fun (the good, clean kind), and when to lead (by example).

Are you the kind of leader you would want to follow? If so, congratulations. But if not, maybe it's time to work on your leadership skills. (Hey, we can all use a little improvement here or there, right?) And a good place to begin is with the words we speak and the example we set.

If you occupy a position of leadership—and officially or unofficially, you do—you should prepare yourself for the day when you'll be faced with a tough, unpopular decision. When that day arrives (and it will probably arrive sooner than you expect), you'll have a choice to make: you can do the right thing or the easy thing.

Do the right thing.

After all, every kitchen heats up on occasion, so you might as well get used to it. And the best way to get used to a warm kitchen is to hang in there and take the heat, knowing that every kitchen, in time, cools down.

> # THE STRENGTH OF THE GROUP IS THE STRENGTH OF THE LEADER.
>
> *Vince Lombardi*

RECAP . . .

You can become a trusted, competent, thoughtful leader if you learn to maintain the right attitude: one that's realistic, optimistic, forward looking, and Christ centered. When it comes to leadership, your actions will speak more loudly than your words.

IN THE HUDDLE

TALK TO your friends about what it means to be a leader at home, at work, and at church. And if you really get your courage up, ask your buddies to assess your leadership skills and offer helpful tips on how you can develop into a stronger leader.

GAME PLAN

LEARN TO follow Jesus before you try to lead others. If you want to be a godly leader, you must first learn to be a faithful follower, a follower of the man from Galilee. Spend some time studying Jesus's leadership style as recorded in the Gospels. Then make a list of ways you can adopt his methods of leadership to enhance your own.

TRUE LEADERS ARE NOT AFRAID TO SURROUND THEMSELVES WITH PEOPLE OF ABILITY—AND NOT AFRAID TO GIVE THOSE PEOPLE OPPORTUNITIES FOR GREATNESS.

Warren Wiersbe

GAME NOTES

An important lesson I learned this week:

_____
_____
_____
_____
_____

What I feel God is telling me this week:

_____
_____
_____
_____
_____

How I'll put this week's game plan into action:

_____
_____
_____
_____
_____
_____
_____
_____
_____
_____
_____
_____

A WORD FROM THE COACH
Don't be obsessed with getting
more material things.
Be relaxed with what you have.
—Hebrews 13:5 MSG

TOO MUCH EQUIPMENT

WARMUPS

- Are you wise enough to stand firm against the temptation to keep acquiring more and more stuff?

- Have you, like so many people in our prosperous society, become ensnared in the trap of materialism?

GOING DEEP

HAVE YOU ever seen a golfer who has thirty-five clubs in his bag but can't hit well with any of them? That's a man with too much equipment and too little ability. On the golf course, as in life, equipment is highly overrated. Don't believe me? Try this mental experiment: Imagine that you give Tiger Woods an old five-iron and a putter, while you get to use the best set of clubs on the market. Then imagine that you and Tiger tee it up in a head-to-head match. Odds are, Tiger will still break par, and you won't come close. The moral of the story? Equipment isn't everything.

IF A PERSON GETS HIS ATTITUDE TOWARD MONEY RIGHT, IT WILL HELP STRAIGHTEN OUT ALMOST EVERY OTHER AREA OF HIS LIFE.

Billy Graham

But the world would have you believe differently.

We live in a world that places a high value on all kinds of equipment, not just golf clubs. It's a society that glorifies stuff, stuff, and more stuff—but that doesn't mean we should glorify stuff too. In fact, the opposite is true.

You've never seen a hearse pulling a U-Haul. As the old saying goes, you can't take it with you. But it sure seems like plenty of us guys are trying.

Whenever we become absorbed in the accumulation of material possessions, trouble is just around the corner. Each new acquisition costs money or time—often both. To further complicate matters, many items can be purchased, not with real money, but with something much more dangerous: debt. Debt—especially credit-card debt—can turn into a modern-day form of indentured servitude.

Perhaps a long string of purchases has hurt your bank balance. If so, it's time to stop the insanity by learning to say no to all the sales pitches trying to convince you that you need to fill up your house with more stuff while, at the same time, you're filling up with more debt.

If you're looking for a surefire way to improve your life, learn to control your possessions before they control you. Ask yourself this simple question: do I own my possessions, or do they own me? If you don't like the answer, make an ironclad promise to stop buying all that stuff! When you do, you'll be amazed at the things you can do without. You'll also be pleasantly surprised at the sense of satisfaction that accompanies your newfound moderation. And you'll understand that when it comes to material possessions, less really is more.

When you finally put all that material stuff in perspective, you can begin storing up riches that will endure throughout eternity—the spiritual kind.

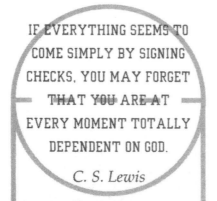

IF EVERYTHING SEEMS TO COME SIMPLY BY SIGNING CHECKS, YOU MAY FORGET THAT YOU ARE AT EVERY MOMENT TOTALLY DEPENDENT ON GOD.

C. S. Lewis

RECAP . . .

The world wants you to believe that money and stuff can buy happiness. Don't buy it! There's absolutely no evidence that material possessions can ensure happiness, but there's plenty of evidence that simplicity and spirituality lead to joy. Genuine happiness comes not from money but from the things money can't buy—starting, of course, with your relationship with God.

IN THE HUDDLE

TALK TO the guys about the futility of keeping up with the Joneses. Discuss whether your spending habits have caused you more harm than good. If you don't like the answers, talk about ways you can spend less and save more and the benefits that could bring to your lives.

GAME PLAN

REASSESS YOUR values. Think long and hard about the priorities and values that guide your decision making, and then map out a plan to help you avoid financial pitfalls. Here are some tips to get you started:

- Purchase only things that make a significant contribution to your well-being and to the well-being of your family.

- Never spend more than you make.

- Never use credit cards as a way of financing your lifestyle.

- Determine an amount to set aside in some sort of savings each week or month—and stick to it!

A SOCIETY THAT PURSUES PLEASURE
RUNS THE RISK OF RAISING EXPECTATIONS EVER HIGHER,
SO THAT TRUE CONTENTMENT
ALWAYS LIES TANTALIZINGLY OUT OF REACH.

Philip Yancey and Paul Brand

GAME NOTES

An important lesson I learned this week:

_____

_____

_____

_____

_____

What I feel God is telling me this week:

_____

_____

_____

_____

_____

How I'll put this week's game plan into action:

_____

_____

_____

_____

_____

_____

_____

_____

_____

_____

_____

A WORD FROM THE COACH
Husbands, go all out in your love for your wives, exactly
as Christ did for the church—a love marked by giving, not
getting. Christ's love makes the church whole.
— *Ephesians 5:25 MSG*

YOU AND YOUR LAWFULLY WEDDED TEAMMATE

WARMUPS

- The Bible says that a wife is to submit to her husband and a husband is to submit to Christ. Which form of submission do you focus on?

- If you're a married man, do you consider your wife to be your best friend, your most trusted advisor, and your eternal traveling partner?

GOING DEEP

OK, NOW I'm going to get personal. Here's the question: how healthy is your marriage? Is it built on the solid foundation of God's love? Do you and your wife strive to be obedient to him as you follow in the footsteps of his Son? If so, you doubtless are the recipient of countless blessings from the Father above. If not, it's time for you and your bride to reevaluate your priorities, your marriage, and your relationship with God.

When you and your wife accept God's love with open arms, you'll be forever changed. Embracing God's love will leave you feeling differently about yourselves, your marriage, your family, and your world. And when you put God first in your lives—including in your marriage—you'll be blessed and protected.

> A SUCCESSFUL MARRIAGE
> IS ALWAYS A
> TRIANGLE: A MAN,
> A WOMAN, AND GOD.
>
> *Cecil Myers*

The apostle Paul taught that men should love their wives the way Christ loves the church. Are you giving this kind of sacrificial love to your wife? If so, you know that your marriage benefits from that unselfish devotion. If not, or if your marriage seems a little less than rock solid, maybe it's time to heed this word of advice: the best way to make love last is by saying "you first" to your wife—and meaning it.

A healthy marriage is an exercise in love, fidelity, trust, forgiveness, encouragement, and teamwork. It requires empathy, tenderness, patience, and perseverance. It is the union of two grownups who consider themselves best friends—friends who are willing to compromise and, when appropriate, to apologize.

A successful marriage requires heaping helpings of common

sense, common courtesy, and uncommon caring. And that's exactly the kind of marriage God has in store for you and your bride if you'll follow him together . . . starting now.

MARITAL LOVE IS A COMMITTED ACT OF THE WILL BEFORE IT IS ANYTHING ELSE. IT IS SACRIFICIAL LOVE, A NO-TURNING-BACK DECISION.

Ed Young

RECAP . . .

Every married man should strive to honor God first and his wife next. Your marriage is too important to build it on shaky ground. But if you build it on the Rock that cannot be moved, you'll be blessed.

IN THE HUDDLE

SHOW ME a husband who's always pointing out that a wife must submit to her husband's authority, and I'll show you a man who has a problem submitting to God's authority. The Bible says that every husband who submits to God's authority will love his wife as Christ loves the church. Discuss this topic with the guys.

GAME PLAN

GIVE GOD a great big thank-you every day. Do you thank God each day for your wife? Perhaps just as important, does your spouse know you're thanking God for her and for your marriage? If so, congratulations—you're a wise man. But if you're not telling your honey that she's the sweetest woman in the world, it's time to warm up your vocal chords and use them appropriately. Whether you're a rookie or a veteran at communicating your affection, brainstorm five fresh ways to tell or show your wife you love and appreciate her, and try them out this week.

A MARITAL RELATIONSHIP THAT ENDURES
AND BECOMES MORE FULFILLING FOR
BOTH THE HUSBAND AND THE WIFE IS NO ACCIDENT.
ONLY HARD WORK MAKES A MARRIAGE MORE FULFILLING.

Gary Smalley

GAME NOTES

An important lesson I learned this week:

_____
_____
_____
_____
_____

What I feel God is telling me this week:

_____
_____
_____
_____
_____
_____

How I'll put this week's game plan into action:

_____
_____
_____
_____
_____
_____
_____
_____
_____
_____
_____
_____

A WORD FROM THE COACH

Never be lazy in your work, but serve
the Lord enthusiastically.

—*Romans 12:11 NLT*

GETTING IN GEAR

WARMUPS

- When you get up in the morning, do you say, "Good morning, Lord!" or "Good Lord, morning"?

- Are you the kind of guy who motivates himself, or do you require a kick in the pants to get yourself in gear?

GOING DEEP

SOMETIMES IT's hard to get motivated, especially when we're not excited about the task at hand. Have you found something that you're passionate about? Does your passion help create a better world for you and for others? If you can answer yes to these questions, you're both fortunate and wise.

Unfortunately, too many men have become intensely passionate about things that improve neither the world nor themselves. They fritter away precious hours in front of the television. Or they may become more interested in their favorite sports team than they are in their chosen profession. Some even fall in love with alcohol, drugs, gambling, or other addictive behaviors that leave little time and energy for anything else.

> WHEN WE REALIZE AND EMBRACE THE LORD'S WILL FOR US, WE WILL LOVE TO DO IT. WE WON'T WANT TO DO ANYTHING ELSE. IT'S A PASSION.
>
> *Franklin Graham*

What are you passionate about that improves your own world and God's world? Have you acquired the habit of doing what needs to be done when it needs to be done, or are you a dues-paying member of the Procrastinators' Club? If you've acquired the habit of doing the right things, and if you've also acquired the habit of doing them sooner rather than later, congratulations! You're running the race well. But if you find yourself goofing off while important work goes undone, it's time to consider the consequences of your behavior and make the necessary course adjustments.

One way you can learn to defeat procrastination is by paying less attention to your fears and more attention to your responsibilities. That's right: procrastination has its roots in fear. So when you're faced with a difficult choice or an unpleasant responsibility, don't spend endless hours fretting over your fate.

Simply seek God's counsel and get busy. When you do, you'll be richly rewarded for your willingness to act.

The world erects no monuments to couch potatoes, so find a worthy cause that inspires and motivates you. Having trouble finding a worthy pursuit that touches your heart and stirs your blood? Ask God to help you, and keep searching until you find it. Trivial Pursuit may be a delightful game to play, but it's a terrible way to live.

> GET ABSOLUTELY ENTHRALLED WITH SOMETHING. THROW YOURSELF INTO IT WITH ABANDON. GET OUT OF YOURSELF. BE SOMEBODY. DO SOMETHING.
>
> *Norman Vincent Peale*

RECAP . . .

There's so much to do and so little time! So we must never wait idly while others do God's work. We, too, must act. Doing God's work is a responsibility each of us must bear; but when we do, our loving heavenly Father rewards our efforts with a bountiful harvest.

IN THE HUDDLE

IT'S TEMPTING to dabble in many things, but if you become a big-time dabbler, you'll inevitably lose focus. In other words, you can either be a big-time dabbler or a big-time doer, but you can't be both. As you think about your own tendencies, talk to your buddies about the difference between dabbling and acting with passion.

GAME PLAN

INCORPORATE HAND-OFFS into your strategy. Think about all the things you're committed to doing, especially the things that take up large blocks of your time. Then rank those activities in order of their importance. Identify the least important activity on your list, and figure out how much time it's taking away from more important tasks. Finally, make concrete plans to hand off your lowest-priority activity to somebody else so you can take immediate action on your most important tasks.

I DON'T SPEND FOREVER ANALYZING THINGS. I GO OUT AND MAKE THINGS HAPPEN.

Dale Earnhardt

GAME NOTES

An important lesson I learned this week:

_____

_____

_____

_____

_____

What I feel God is telling me this week:

_____

_____

_____

_____

_____

How I'll put this week's game plan into action:

_____

_____

_____

_____

_____

_____

_____

_____

_____

_____

_____

A WORD FROM THE COACH
Be joyful always; pray continually; give
thanks in all circumstances, for this
is God's will for you in Christ Jesus.
—1 Thessalonians 5:16–18 NIV

TIME-OUT FOR THANKSGIVING

WARMUPS

- When was the last time you counted your blessings?

    a. A few minutes ago
    b. Yesterday
    c. Last week
    d. Can't remember

GOING DEEP

HERE'S A simple concept that's guaranteed to make you a winner: if you want to get the most out of life, cultivate a thankful heart. How? One way is by taking a time-out to meditate on all you have to be thankful for.

Are you the kind of guy who counts his blessings instead of his problems? Do you appreciate the gifts God has given you and the life you're privileged to live? When you stop to think about it, God has given you more blessings than you can count; you most certainly should be thankful. So the question of the day is this: will you slow down long enough to thank your heavenly Father or just keep rushing along, living life without gratitude?

> WHEN IT COMES TO LIFE, THE CRITICAL THING IS WHETHER YOU TAKE THINGS FOR GRANTED OR TAKE THEM WITH GRATITUDE.
>
> *G. K. Chesterton*

Some of you are probably thinking, *It's easy for the Swan to talk about slowing down, but I have a lot to do!* Well, of course you do, but that still doesn't make you exempt from God's commandments. And God has commanded us—even with our busy schedules—to take time to praise him and give thanks for his blessings.

Sometimes life can be complicated and demanding. And when those demands leave us rushing from place to place with scarcely a moment to spare, it's easy to forget to pause and thank our Creator for the countless blessings he has given us and our families. Failing to thank God is understandable . . . but wrong.

A wise heart is a thankful heart. Your heavenly Father has blessed you beyond measure, and you owe him everything, starting with your gratitude. God is always listening—are you willing to say thanks?

GOD'S KINDNESS IS NOT LIKE
THE SUNSET—BRILLIANT
IN ITS INTENSITY, BUT
DYING EVERY SECOND. GOD'S
GENEROSITY KEEPS COMING
AND COMING AND COMING.

Bill Hybels

RECAP...

God gives each of us more blessings than we can count. Those blessings include life, family, freedom, friends, talents, and possessions, just for starters. Winners recognize the size and scope of God's blessings—and real winners (like you) spend plenty of time thanking him.

IN THE HUDDLE

TALK TO your buddies about how glad you are to be where you are in your life and about the ways God has richly blessed all of you. Discuss your blessings in light of the situations of less fortunate people around the world. Then ask yourselves what you should do in response to God's gifts.

GAME PLAN

START KEEPING score. Start counting your blessings, that is. You'll discover that you really have too many to list, but it never hurts to try. Each day this week write down five things—different things, no repeats—you have to be thankful for. Then, next time you feel blue, look over your old "scorecards" . . . and start a few new ones. You'll soon recognize how blessed you really are.

CONTENTMENT COMES WHEN WE DEVELOP AN ATTITUDE OF GRATITUDE FOR THE IMPORTANT THINGS WE DO HAVE IN OUR LIVES THAT WE TEND TO TAKE FOR GRANTED.

Dave Ramsey

GAME NOTES

An important lesson I learned this week:

_____
_____
_____
_____
_____

What I feel God is telling me this week:

_____
_____
_____
_____
_____

How I'll put this week's game plan into action:

_____
_____
_____
_____
_____
_____
_____
_____
_____
_____
_____

A WORD FROM THE COACH

If anyone wants to come with Me,
he must deny himself,
take up his cross daily, and follow Me.

—*Luke 9:23 HCSB*

GETTING IN STEP

WARMUPS

- Are you following Jesus as closely as you can, or are you lagging so far behind that you can hardly see him from where you are?

- Are you radically different because of your relationship with Jesus, or are you the same person you were before you invited him into your life?

- Are you willing to follow Christ wherever he chooses to lead, or will you only allow him to lead you in the direction you've already decided to go?

GOING DEEP

IF YOU'RE absolutely convinced that you're on the exact path Jesus has called you to follow, feel free to put down this book and pick up the sports page. But if you're less than 100 percent certain (like most of us) that you're faithfully following in the Master's footsteps, read on.

An old hymn begins, "What a friend we have in Jesus . . ." No truer words were ever penned. Jesus is the sovereign friend and ultimate savior of mankind. Why did Christ endure the humiliation and torture of the cross? He did it for you. He showed enduring love for you by willingly sacrificing his own life so that you might have eternal life. And his love is as near as your next breath, as personal as your next thought, more essential than your next heartbeat.

> ONLY BY WALKING WITH GOD CAN WE HOPE TO FIND THE PATH THAT LEADS TO LIFE.
>
> *John Eldredge*

What can you do in response to his gifts? Accept his love, praise his name, and share his message. And conduct yourself in a manner that demonstrates to all the world that your acquaintance with the Master is not a passing fad but rather the cornerstone and touchstone of your life.

On whose team will you choose to play today? Will you join with shortsighted people who play by the world's rules, or will you join league with the Son of God? Jesus is rooting for you. Hopefully, you will choose to be on his team today and every day of your life. When you do, God's Word promises that you will learn how to live "freely and lightly" (Matthew 11:28–30 MSG).

Jesus doesn't want you to be a run-of-the-mill, follow-the-crowd kind of guy. He wants you to be a "new creation" through him (2 Corinthians 5:17 NIV). And that's what you should want for yourself too. Nothing is more important than your wholehearted commitment to your Creator and to his only Son. Your faith must never be merely the halftime show; it must be your whole game—your ultimate priority and your ultimate passion. Anything less falls short of the goal.

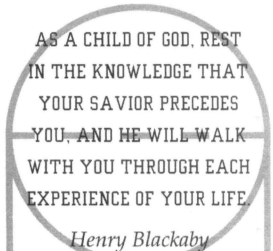

AS A CHILD OF GOD, REST IN THE KNOWLEDGE THAT YOUR SAVIOR PRECEDES YOU, AND HE WILL WALK WITH YOU THROUGH EACH EXPERIENCE OF YOUR LIFE.

Henry Blackaby

RECAP . . .

You are the recipient of Christ's love. Accept it enthusiastically and share it passionately. Jesus deserves your wholehearted commitment, and when you give it, you'll receive his wholehearted reward.

IN THE HUDDLE

TALK TO your friends about what it means to follow Jesus. The Christian life should be a triumphal celebration, a daily exercise in thanksgiving and praise. Discuss ways you can live out that celebration, then share it with other friends who haven't yet experienced it.

GAME PLAN

STUDY THE numbers to see how much time you spend playing for the world's team and how much for God's. Pull out a pencil and paper, and take time to study how you spend a typical day. Try to figure out what percentage of your life is spent meeting the world's expectations and obligations, and what percentage you're investing in God's work. Then, if you don't like the numbers you see, take steps today to improve your winning percentage by reviewing your priorities and redoing your to-do list.

IN ALL YOUR DEEDS AND WORDS, YOU SHOULD LOOK ON JESUS AS YOUR MODEL, WHETHER YOU ARE KEEPING SILENCE OR SPEAKING, WHETHER YOU ARE ALONE OR WITH OTHERS.

Saint Bonaventure

GAME NOTES

An important lesson I learned this week:

_____

_____

_____

_____

What I feel God is telling me this week:

_____

_____

_____

_____

_____

How I'll put this week's game plan into action:

_____

_____

_____

_____

_____

_____

_____

_____

_____

_____

A WORD FROM THE COACH

When a man is gloomy, everything seems to go wrong;
when he is cheerful, everything seems right!
—*Proverbs 15:15 TLB*

UNSPORTSMANLIKE CONDUCT

WARMUPS

- How do you react to life's frustrations?
- Do you allow your thoughts to be hijacked by the negativity that seems to dominate our troubled world?
- Are you fearful, angry, bored, or just plain grumpy? Or are you determined to enjoy God's gift of life?

GOING DEEP

SOME GUYS have raised grumpiness to an art form (albeit a decidedly unattractive art form). And some find ways to complain about almost everything (while putting forth few solutions . . . and taking even fewer actions to solve the problems).

Hey, it's easy, and sometimes pretty tempting, to complain. But that's not the way God wants us to play the game of life. Don't allow yourself to become a member of the Grumpy Old Men's Club.

Few things are sadder or, for that matter, more absurd than a person griping and complaining his way through life. Christ offers us joy, but he won't force us to be cheery. We must claim his gift of joy for ourselves. But sometimes we're slow to do so. Why is that? Why would anyone not reach out and grab as much joy as possible?

Because as imperfect human beings, we often lose sight of our blessings. Ironically, most of us have more good things in our lives than we can count, yet we still find reasons to complain about the minor frustrations of everyday life. That's not only unhelpful, but it's the pinnacle of shortsightedness and a serious roadblock on the path to spiritual abundance—because the penalty for our "unsportsmanlike conduct" is that we miss out on some great teamwork and victories with our fellow players, not to mention kudos from the Coach.

> IT IS NOT FITTING, WHEN ONE IS IN GOD'S SERVICE, TO HAVE A GLOOMY FACE OR A CHILLING LOOK.
>
> *Saint Francis of Assisi*

If you've allowed frustration to throw you off your game, try this: pray for wisdom, for patience, and for a heart that is so filled with gratitude and forgiveness that it has no room for grouchiness. God will help you cut the crankiness if you ask him—and if you let him. And that's a good thing, because grumpiness and peace cannot coexist in the same mind.

So next time you find yourself feeling surlier than a sidelined superstar, remember God's blessings and redirect your thoughts, focusing on the good in your life instead of the bad. This world is God's creation; look for the best in it, and trust him to take care of the rest.

THE GREATEST SIGN
OF WISDOM IS CONTINUED
CHEERFULNESS.

Michel de Montaigne

RECAP . . .

Sometimes even the most cheerful of us can become grumpy. But grumpiness is not God's way. Our heavenly Father is a God of possibility, not negativity—and you should strive to be a man who focuses on life's potential, not its setbacks.

IN THE HUDDLE

HAPPINESS IS contagious—but so are negative emotions. Talk to your buddies about the way one man's grumpiness can affect his workplace and his family. Then think carefully about how your own attitude impacts your coworkers and family members.

GAME PLAN

PUT MOODINESS under the microscope. Think about the last time you found yourself in a seriously bad mood. Consider what may have caused your moodiness. Were you exhausted? Overcommitted? Stressed? Disappointed with yourself? Had you skipped your daily devotional time? Make notes about the things that can predictably put you in the emotional penalty box. Brainstorm ways to avoid the behaviors that usually lead to unsportsmanlike conduct.

THE PEOPLE WHOM I HAVE SEEN SUCCEED BEST IN LIFE HAVE ALWAYS BEEN CHEERFUL AND HOPEFUL PEOPLE WHO WENT ABOUT THEIR BUSINESS WITH A SMILE ON THEIR FACES.

Charles Kingsley

GAME NOTES

An important lesson I learned this week:

_____
_____
_____
_____
_____

What I feel God is telling me this week:

_____
_____
_____
_____
_____

How I'll put this week's game plan into action:

_____
_____
_____
_____
_____
_____
_____
_____
_____
_____
_____
_____

PERSONAL TRAINING

WARMUPS

- Consider the man you are today as compared with the man you were a year ago, then five years ago. How have you grown through your experiences?

- How have you profited from your mistakes?

- How can you continue to learn, to grow, and to improve yourself?

GOING DEEP

IF YOU'RE like me, you've grown quite a lot over the past few years . . . around the middle! But what about your spiritual growth? Is the size of your heart growing at least as quickly as the size of your belt? Hopefully so. After all, God doesn't want you to get soft. He wants you to stay in shape . . . spiritually and physically.

The training that builds us up toward spiritual maturity takes a lifetime. We can and should continue to grow in the love and knowledge of God as long as we live. Norman Vincent Peale had the following advice: "Ask the God who made you to keep remaking you." Dr. Peale's advice was right on the money. It's never too late to learn and to grow, and God is the best personal trainer there is.

In 1902 a fifty-two-year-old milkshake-mixer salesman named Ray Kroc discovered a small but promising chain of four restaurants that made great hamburgers and tasty fries. That little company was McDonald's, which Kroc promptly bought. With his leadership and vision it became the largest restaurant chain in

> **NEVER BE AFRAID TO RE-CREATE YOURSELF.**
>
> *George Foreman*

the world. When asked about growth— both corporate and personal—Kroc said, "When you're green, you're growing; when you're ripe, you rot." Even in his fifties, Kroc was still "green," and the rest of us should take note. It's almost never too late to launch out into some new, exciting phase of our lives.

But when we stop developing and let ourselves get out of shape, either emotionally or spiritually, we do ourselves a big disservice. There's no steroid to pump up our souls, but if we do the spiritual workouts of studying God's Word, obeying his commandments, and living in the center of his will, we won't become spiritually flabby.

We'll be vital, healthy men of faith . . . and that's exactly what God intends for us to be.

Of course, as in any regimen, we all eventually plateau. And just as pushing past a physical plateau can be tough, so many of life's most important challenges are difficult to overcome. But that's exactly when we need to stay focused and persevere—keep our eyes and our hearts open to God's instruction, knowing that our faith exercises will pay off in the end.

The Bible promises this: tough times are temporary, but God's love is not—it lasts forever. Your heavenly Father is always standing right beside you, ready to help you to the next level.

PROGRESS AND
IMPROVEMENT DO NOT
COME IN BIG BUNCHES;
THEY COME IN
LITTLE PIECES.

Arthur Ashe

RECAP . . .

Life is a series of choices. Each day you make countless decisions that can bring you closer to God . . . or lead you away from him. When you stick to the spiritual discipline of living according to God's laws, seeking his will, and studying his Word, you'll build spiritual muscle that can, and should, last a lifetime.

IN THE HUDDLE

YOU PROBABLY have friends who always seem to stay in shape and keep developing—spiritually, mentally, emotionally, and professionally. And you also know guys who seem a little soft or stuck at a certain level. Talk to your buddies about what exercises might lead to increased spiritual and personal strength. And discuss how you can "spot" each other when life's challenges make for heavy lifting.

GAME PLAN

FIGHT SPIRITUAL flabbiness. Even if you're a fine, God-fearing fellow, you've still got plenty of room for improvement. So here's a challenge: Pull out a blank sheet of paper and a pencil, and write down at least three things you can do to become more spiritually fit. Then jot down exactly what you're going to do about it. Next, sign and date the page, committing—to yourself and your Creator—to strengthen your spiritual health. Let the workout begin.

A CHRISTIAN IS NEVER IN A STATE OF COMPLETION BUT ALWAYS IN THE PROCESS OF BECOMING.

Martin Luther

GAME NOTES

An important lesson I learned this week:

_____

_____

_____

_____

_____

What I feel God is telling me this week:

_____

_____

_____

_____

_____

_____

How I'll put this week's game plan into action:

_____

_____

_____

_____

_____

_____

_____

_____

_____

_____

_____

_____

A WORD FROM THE COACH
Don't worry about tomorrow, because tomorrow will worry about itself. Each day has enough trouble of its own.
—*Matthew 6:34 HCSB*

ONLY A GAME

WARMUPS

- As you're playing the game of life, do you worry endlessly about the score?

- Are you so anxious about the future that you forget to enjoy the present?

- If you're overly anxious, are you really trusting God?

GOING DEEP

IN THE game of life, you win some and you lose some. Living is risky business; ours is an uncertain world, one in which trouble may come calling at any moment. No wonder we feel a little panicky at times.

Are you one of those fellows who sometimes spends more time worrying about a problem than you spend solving it? If so, here's a great strategy for dealing with your worries: take them to God. Take your troubles to him; take your fears to him; take your doubts to him; take your weaknesses to him; take your sorrows to him . . . and leave them all there. Period.

> IT IS IMPOSSIBLE FOR THAT MAN TO DESPAIR WHO REMEMBERS THAT HIS HELPER IS OMNIPOTENT.
>
> *Jeremy Taylor*

Because none of us is perfect, it's almost impossible for us to have perfect trust in God. So, when faced with the struggles and hardships of life, we worry. Even though we have the promise of God's love and protection, we find ourselves fretting over the inevitable frustrations we encounter. Jesus understood our concerns when he spoke the reassuring words found in the sixth chapter of Matthew.

The more we learn to trust God, the less we'll find to worry about. And the more we learn to see the world from God's perspective, the less concerned we'll be about the inevitable ups and downs of everyday life.

Perhaps you're troubled about your future, your health, or your finances. Or perhaps you are simply a worrier by nature. Either way, make it a point to read Matthew 6:25–34 once each day this week. This beautiful passage will remind you that God still sits on the throne in his heaven, and you are his beloved child. Then, perhaps, you can worry a little less and trust

God a little more. And that's as it should be, because God is
trustworthy . . . he's got you covered!

WORRY IS SIMPLY THINKING
THE SAME THING OVER AND
OVER AGAIN . . . AND NOT
DOING ANYTHING ABOUT IT.

Branch Rickey

RECAP . . .

*If you're a man with lots of obligations and plenty of
responsibilities, it's probably a simple fact of life that sometimes
you worry. What to do with those concerns? Take them to God.
Seek protection from the One who offers you eternal love and
protection; build your spiritual house on the Rock that cannot
be moved.*

IN THE HUDDLE

ASK YOUR buddies whether they think it's better to worry about problems or to do the hard work of solving them. The answer should be obvious. Now discuss ways you can switch from anxiety to action. Next time you find yourself worrying instead of working, use those tips to help you get busy doing what you can to solve your problem—and trust God to take care of the rest.

GAME PLAN

CONTROL YOUR worries about uncontrollable problems. Divide your worries into two categories: those you can control and those you cannot. Make an action plan to deal with the first list, then promise yourself that you won't waste time or energy worrying about the second list. Remember: today is the tomorrow you worried about yesterday.

THE BEGINNING OF ANXIETY IS THE END OF FAITH, AND THE BEGINNING OF TRUE FAITH IS THE END OF ANXIETY.

George Mueller

GAME NOTES

An important lesson I learned this week:

_____
_____
_____
_____
_____

What I feel God is telling me this week:

_____
_____
_____
_____
_____

How I'll put this week's game plan into action:

_____
_____
_____
_____
_____
_____
_____
_____
_____
_____

A WORD FROM THE COACH

Your attitude should be the same as that
of Christ Jesus: Who, being in very nature
God, did not consider equality with
God something to be grasped, but made
himself nothing, taking the very nature of
a servant, being made in human likeness.
And being found in appearance as a man,
he humbled himself and became obedient
to death—even death on a cross!
—*Philippians 2:5–8 NIV*

TONING YOUR 'TUDE

WARMUPS

- On the wall of a little donut shop, the sign read:

    As you travel through life, brother,
    Whatever be your goal,
    Keep your eye upon the donut,
    And not upon the hole.

- Have you acquired the bad habit of looking only at the hole?

- How might your life be better if you could "keep your eye upon the donut"?

GOING DEEP

WHETHER YOU realize it or not, your attitude is a choice. As the simple rhyme on the previous page points out, you can choose to look at the donut or the hole. And it's a decision only you can make.

When you stop to think about it, life is a big, long string of choices. From the instant we wake up in the morning until the moment we nod off to sleep at night, we make countless decisions: decisions about the things we do, decisions about the words we speak, and decisions about our attitude. Simply put, the quality of those decisions, to a large extent, determines the quality of our lives.

> WHEN YOU GET RIGHT DOWN TO THE WOOD CHOPPING, THE KEY TO WINNING IS CONFIDENCE.
>
> *Darrell Royal*

Irving Berlin, the man who wrote "God Bless America" and "White Christmas," once observed, "Life is ten percent how you make it and ninety percent how you take it." Berlin understood that in life, the right attitude is crucial. So if you've become caught up in the daily grind, step back, compose your thoughts, and count your blessings.

As a man who's the recipient of gifts from a loving and merciful God, you have every reason to choose a positive attitude. Even so, with all the hustle and bustle of life, sometimes it's all too easy to choose a less-than-positive attitude. If you give in to that temptation, however, you risk forfeiting the joy and peace that might otherwise have been yours.

It's up to you to think optimistically about your life, your profession, your family, your future, and your purpose for living. It's up to you to embrace your dreams, not your fears. It's up to you to take time to celebrate God's glorious creation. Sure, some days that might take a little extra effort.

But when you do, you'll find your heart filled with hope and gladness. Then it's simply up to you to share your optimism with others.

So here's a tip from your old pal the Swan: don't sweat the small stuff. And when it comes to life here on earth, everything that doesn't pertain to your relationship with your heavenly Father is, relatively speaking, the small stuff.

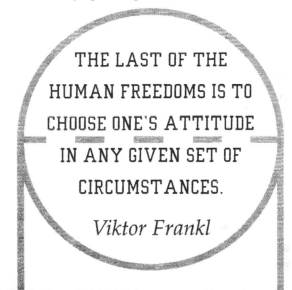

THE LAST OF THE
HUMAN FREEDOMS IS TO
CHOOSE ONE'S ATTITUDE
IN ANY GIVEN SET OF
CIRCUMSTANCES.

Viktor Frankl

RECAP . . .

Because you're a human being, you're always thinking about something. You simply can't help yourself: your brain never shuts off, even when you're asleep. But you can use your thoughts to help make your life better when you adopt an attitude that focuses on your blessings, not your misfortunes. Do yourself and your loved ones a favor: learn to think optimistically about the world you live in and the life you lead. Then get ready to enjoy the rewards your positive attitude will bring.

IN THE HUDDLE

NEXT TIME you're chatting with the guys, pay attention to the mood. Is it upbeat and positive? I'll bet you feel better when you're hanging out with fellows who choose to look at the sunny side of life. You've heard the saying "Life is what you make it." That means you have a choice. You and your buddies can choose to have a life full of frustration and fear, or you can just as easily choose one of joy and contentment. The correct choice should be obvious!

GAME PLAN

REVIEW YOUR *"game tapes."* Take a few minutes to think about the last time you let a negative attitude take control of your day. Then write down a detailed account. First, describe the situation. Next, jot down a few ideas about where you went wrong: Were you exhausted? Did you focus on the hole instead of the donut? Did you allow yourself to become "infected" by somebody else's negative attitude? Finally, write down ways to handle the same situation the next time it happens (which, by the way, it will).

MORALE AND ATTITUDE ARE THE FUNDAMENTAL INGREDIENTS TO SUCCESS.

Bud Wilkinson

GAME NOTES

An important lesson I learned this week:

_____

_____

_____

_____

_____

What I feel God is telling me this week:

_____

_____

_____

_____

_____

How I'll put this week's game plan into action:

_____

_____

_____

_____

_____

_____

_____

_____

_____

_____

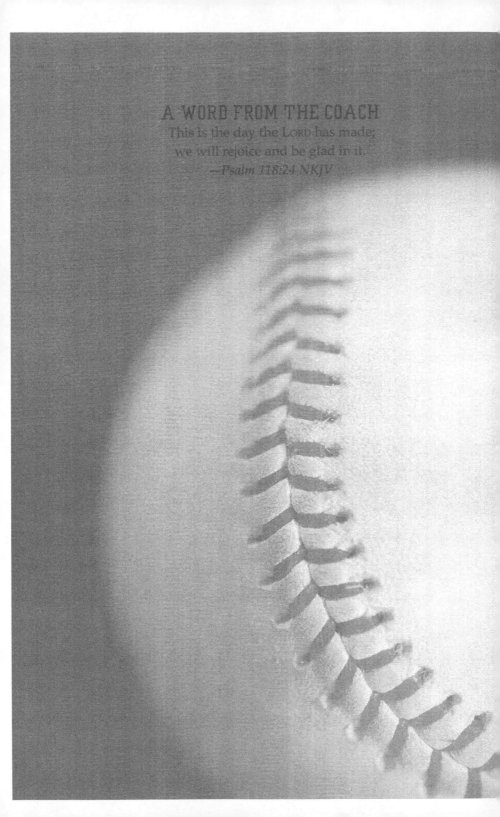

A WORD FROM THE COACH
This is the day the LORD has made;
we will rejoice and be glad in it.
—*Psalm 118:24 NKJV*

PLAYING TWO

WARMUPS

- What do you expect from the day ahead?
- Are you expecting God to do wonderful things, or are you living beneath a cloud of apprehension and doubt?
- Are you willing to really celebrate life?

GOING DEEP

THE GREAT Chicago Cubs shortstop Ernie Banks understood how blessed he was to be a professional ballplayer stationed in the friendly confines of historic Wrigley Field. That's why Ernie's favorite saying was "Let's play two." For Mr. Cub, one baseball game a day was cause for celebration, but two was twice as much fun.

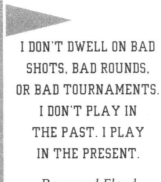

I DON'T DWELL ON BAD SHOTS, BAD ROUNDS, OR BAD TOURNAMENTS. I DON'T PLAY IN THE PAST. I PLAY IN THE PRESENT.

Raymond Floyd

Are you like Ernie Banks? Do you look at the game of life as a great big cause for celebration? Do you view every new sunrise as a fresh opportunity to thank the good Lord for everything he's done for you in the past and everything he has promised to do for you throughout eternity? If so, you're to be congratulated . . . if not, maybe you're in need of an extreme spiritual makeover!

What do you expect from the day ahead? Do you expect God to use you in surprising ways, or do you expect another uneventful day filled with the same old, same old?

Charles H. Spurgeon, the nineteenth-century English clergyman, advised, "Rejoicing is clearly a spiritual command. To ignore it, I need to remind you, is disobedience." We are called by our Creator to live abundantly, prayerfully, and joyfully. To do otherwise is to squander his spiritual gifts.

Christ came to earth to give us abundant life and eternal salvation. Our task is to accept his grace with joy in our hearts and praise on our lips. When we plan our days around Jesus, we see the world differently, we act differently, and we feel differently about ourselves and our neighbors.

If you're a thoughtful man of faith, then you're a thankful

man of faith. And because of your faith, you can face the inevitable challenges and disappointments of each day armed with the joy of Christ and the promise of salvation.

So whatever this day holds for you, begin it and end it with God as your partner. And throughout the day, give thanks to the One who created you and saved you. God's love for you is infinite—accept it joyfully and be thankful.

EVERY DAY SHOULD BE A
FANTASTIC ADVENTURE
FOR US BECAUSE WE'RE
IN THE MIDDLE OF
GOD'S UNFOLDING PLAN
FOR THE AGES.

John MacArthur

RECAP . . .

God offers you life, eternal and abundant. If that doesn't seem to you like cause for celebration, maybe it's time to think again about all the gifts you've received from God. When you do, you'll naturally want to "play two"—celebrate and thank him for his blessings.

IN THE HUDDLE

TALK TO your friends about the past, the present, and the future. Yesterday is gone; tomorrow is yet to arrive. But you do have today. Make sure you and your pals enjoy this day . . . compliments of God.

GAME PLAN

MAKE TODAY your gift to God. Every day is a glorious opportunity to place yourself in the service of the One who is the giver of all blessings. When you celebrate God's gifts—when you keep God's promises firmly in your mind and your heart—you'll find yourself celebrating life. And that's exactly what God wants you to do.

WHEREVER YOU ARE, BE ALL THERE. LIVE TO THE HILT EVERY SITUATION YOU BELIEVE TO BE THE WILL OF GOD.

Jim Elliot

GAME NOTES

An important lesson I learned this week:

_____

_____

_____

_____

_____

What I feel God is telling me this week:

_____

_____

_____

_____

_____

How I'll put this week's game plan into action:

_____

_____

_____

_____

_____

_____

_____

_____

_____

_____

_____

A WORD FROM THE COACH

My soul thirsts for God, for the living God.

—*Psalm 42:2 NASB*

CROWD PLEASER OR GOD PLEASER?

WARMUPS

- From whom do you seek approval?
- Whom will you try to please: God or society?
- Whom will you choose to follow today: your peers or your God?

GOING DEEP

ASK ANY star athlete, and he or she will probably tell you that there's no feeling quite like receiving a standing ovation from an enthusiastic home crowd. And like any big-time playmaker, you, too, want to be appreciated—by your family, by your friends, by your coworkers, and by your boss, to name only a few.

And why shouldn't you want a little appreciation? After all, you're out there in the trenches giving it everything you've got. It's only natural for you to hope that your home crowd notices. But here's something to think about: if you spend too much time and energy playing to the audience, you might start doing things that displease your heavenly Father—and if you do, you're heading straight for trouble.

> THERE IS NOTHING THAT MAKES MORE COWARDS AND FEEBLE MEN THAN PUBLIC OPINION.
>
> *Henry Ward Beecher*

Why is it so tempting to ham it up in front of your friends and neighbors? Well, think about it: You live in a highly competitive world, a place where far too many of your contemporaries are struggling to be noticed and appreciated. Many of these folks are not particularly concerned about being noticed by God (if, in fact, they think about God at all). Instead, they want to be noticed by the world. And because you're competing alongside these people, you may find it tempting to play to the crowd right along with them. But resist that temptation. God doesn't want you to be a chest-thumping prima donna. He wants you to be a humble servant, and that's exactly what you should strive to become.

Rick Warren observed, "Those who follow the crowd usually get lost in it." He might well have added that those who play to the crowd usually pay for their shortsightedness. So forget about being a crowd pleaser, and concentrate, instead, on being a God-fearing, God-praising, God-pleasing man. When you learn to rein in your ego, you'll be doing everybody a big favor, especially yourself. So here's a timeless tip, compliments of the Swan: don't seek status; seek God. If you can follow that strategy every day of your life, you'll be happy and blessed.

YOU SHOULD FORGET
ABOUT TRYING TO BE
POPULAR WITH EVERYBODY
AND START TRYING
TO BE POPULAR WITH
GOD ALMIGHTY.

Sam Jones

RECAP . . .

We all seek approval—the big question is from whom? Some guys look to the world as a source of popularity and approval. Wise men seek to please God. If you want to please God, you certainly won't have any trouble finding him. When you earnestly seek God, you will find him, because he's right there, waiting patiently for you to reach out to him. And make no mistake: your soul does, indeed, thirst for God. That thirst was planted in your heart by the Creator, and it's a thirst only he can quench. Let him—right here . . . right now.

IN THE HUDDLE

TALK TO the guys about the trap of trying to please people instead of God. Discuss the perceived need to impress your neighbors versus the genuine need to please your Creator. Talk about the wisdom of humility and the folly of pride. And while you're at it, encourage everyone in your group to reread Proverbs, a book that has a lot to say about the need to stay humble and put God first.

GAME PLAN

A THINKING man doesn't follow the crowd. He follows Jesus. What is your focus today? Is it on seeking God and pleasing him, or is it on making sure you're well liked by those in your professional and social circles? Remember: it's impossible to please everybody, but it's not impossible to please God. So please him first, and everything else will have a way of taking care of itself.

PEOPLE WHO CONSTANTLY, AND FERVENTLY, SEEK THE APPROVAL OF OTHERS LIVE WITH AN IDENTITY CRISIS. THEY DON'T KNOW WHO THEY ARE, AND THEY ARE DEFINED BY WHAT OTHERS THINK OF THEM.

Charles Stanley

GAME NOTES

An important lesson I learned this week:

_____
_____
_____
_____
_____

What I feel God is telling me this week:

_____
_____
_____
_____
_____

How I'll put this week's game plan into action:

_____
_____
_____
_____
_____
_____
_____
_____
_____
_____
_____

RUNNING FROM TEMPTATION

WARMUPS

- What steps are you taking to avoid temptations that have the potential to destroy your life?

- Are you taking your mind, your heart, and your body to places that honor God, or are you spending time with people and in atmospheres that might lead you astray?

GOING DEEP

EVERYWHERE YOU turn, or so it seems, you can get into big trouble. This world is filled to the brim with temptations. Some of those temptations are small, like eating a second order of French fries—yep, it's mighty tempting to ask the waitress for a second helping with extra salt and a fresh bottle of catsup—tempting, but not too dangerous. Other temptations, however, aren't quite so harmless.

Our enemy, the devil, is working around the clock to cause pain and heartache in more ways than ever before. We men must remain watchful and strong. But the good news is this: When it comes to fighting Satan, we're never alone. God is always with us, and he gives us the power to resist temptation whenever we ask him for that strength.

> THE HIGHER THE HILL, THE STRONGER THE WIND: SO THE LOFTIER THE LIFE, THE STRONGER THE ENEMY'S TEMPTATIONS.
>
> *John Wycliffe*

When we weave the habit of prayer into the fabric of our days, when we sincerely ask God to deliver us from evil, he will do it. When we consult God on an hourly basis, we avail ourselves of his wisdom, his power, and his love. But nobody is going to force you to ask God for help. You must ask him yourself.

In a letter to fellow followers of Jesus, the apostle Peter offered a stern warning: "Your adversary, the devil, prowls around like a roaring lion, seeking someone to devour" (1 Peter 5:8 NASB). What was true in New Testament times is equally true in our own. Satan tempts his prey and then devours them. And it's up to you—and only you—to make sure you're not one of those being devoured!

We must be on our guard, because temptations are everywhere. Satan is determined to win; we must be equally determined not to let him.

THE SOUL POSSESSES
FREEDOM; AND THOUGH
THE DEVIL CAN MAKE
SUGGESTIONS, HE DOESN'T
HAVE THE POWER
TO COMPEL YOU AGAINST
YOUR WILL.

Saint Cyril of Jerusalem

RECAP . . .

*When you encounter the evils of this world—and you will—
use prayer as an antidote and common sense as your guide.
Turn your temptations over to a Power much greater than
your own. And be comforted by the certainty that no challenge
is too great for God.*

IN THE HUDDLE

TEMPTATION HAS different effects on different people. Talk to your friends about the people, places, and things they struggle with, and share what situations can trap you in a hurry. Then talk about precautions you can take to make sure you avoid the devil's handiwork.

GAME PLAN

USE THE Bible as your blueprint for life and your shield against temptation. After fasting forty days and nights in the desert, Jesus himself was tempted by Satan. Christ used Scripture to rebuke the devil (read Matthew 4:1–11), and you can do likewise. The Bible provides you with a blueprint for righteous living. Consult it daily, and follow it carefully. Then you'll be safe from the enemy's snare.

IN TIMES OF TEMPTATION THERE IS ONE COMMAND: FLEE! GET AWAY FROM IT, FOR EVERY STRUGGLE AGAINST LUST USING ONLY ONE'S OWN STRENGTH IS DOOMED TO FAILURE.

Dietrich Bonhoeffer

GAME NOTES

An important lesson I learned this week:

_____

_____

_____

_____

_____

What I feel God is telling me this week:

_____

_____

_____

_____

_____

How I'll put this week's game plan into action:

_____

_____

_____

_____

_____

_____

_____

_____

_____

_____

_____

A WORD FROM THE COACH

Keep your eyes focused on what is right, and look
straight ahead to what is good. Be careful what
you do, and always do what is right. Don't turn off
the road of goodness; keep away from evil paths.

—*Proverbs 4:25–27 NCV*

CHALK TALK

WARMUPS

- As you get ready for the day ahead, are you willing to concentrate on a few fundamentals that have the potential to jump-start your day and your life?

- Do you see today as an opportunity to achieve major-league success by focusing on the fundamentals, or are your thoughts (and plans) so scattered that you're just jumping around from place to place?

GOING DEEP

OK, BIG fella, you don't have to be a Phi Beta Kappa to see that we're getting down to the end of this playbook, and fast. That means it's the perfect time to engage in a time-honored sports tradition: the chalk talk. So let's pull out our imaginary blackboard (complete with squeaky chalk and dusty erasers) and sum up a few fundamental points before you head out to play your next big game:

1. *Focus on God.* If you put your obligations to other people (or your desire for stuff) above your desire to please God, you're making a king-sized mistake. So as you're making plans for the day ahead, put God in the top slot. When you do, you'll make better choices—and reap the rewards.

2. *Focus on getting your attitude right.* If you let yourself fall victim to stinkin' thinkin', you'll never get ahead. So if you want to be a winner, make sure your attitude enhances your chances of success.

3. *Focus on your game plan.* By this time, hopefully, you've developed a solid game plan. Now it's time to execute that plan with intensity and determination.

4. *Focus on your work, not your worries.* Worry is never a valid substitute for work. So get out there, do your best, and turn your worries over to God.

5. *Enjoy the game today.* You're on the playing field today, but there's no guarantee you'll be there tomorrow—so have fun now. Besides, you'll always play better when you play happy.

As your old high-school coach used to say, it's all about the fundamentals. So as you head out onto the playing fields of life, keep your eyes on the big prizes and focus on doing a few fundamental things right. When you do, you'll increase your chances of winning big victories for your family, for yourself, for your community, and for your Creator. And then you'll have won the biggest victory there is.

FIRST, MASTER THE
FUNDAMENTALS.

Larry Bird

RECAP . . .

If you want to be a winner, don't keep too many competing ideas rattling around in your brain. Focus, instead, on a few powerful keys to success, and hammer those points home again and again until victory is yours.

IN THE HUDDLE

HAVE A chalk talk with your buddies about the need to focus on a few fundamental keys to success. Examine the drawbacks of disorganization and the disadvantages of being scattered. And while you're at it, talk specifically about things you can and should do to sharpen your focus for the days and weeks ahead.

GAME PLAN

Focus on your own fundamentals. Think about your strengths and weaknesses. Then jot down two or three fundamentals that apply to you—two or three steps you can take (or the habits you can acquire) that will help you reach your goals. After you've clearly identified your own fundamental keys to success, focus on them relentlessly . . . and keep focusing as long as you play the game.

THE MOST SUCCESSFUL COACHES
ON ANY LEVEL TEACH THE FUNDAMENTALS.

John McKay

GAME NOTES

An important lesson I learned this week:

_____
_____
_____
_____
_____

What I feel God is telling me this week:

_____
_____
_____
_____
_____

How I'll put this week's game plan into action:

_____
_____
_____
_____
_____
_____
_____
_____
_____
_____
_____

ABOUT THE AUTHOR

DR. DENNIS Swanberg, affectionately known to his national TV audiences as "the Swan," is a seasoned and solid communicator whose sly wit delivers life-enriching truths to the heart on wings of laughter. Swanberg is a well-qualified teacher, speaker, counselor, minister, and TV host. He holds a BA in Greek/Religion from Baylor University and a doctorate in divinity/ministry from Southwestern Baptist Theological Seminary. *The Dennis Swanberg Show* and *Swan's Place*, his nationally televised shows, are viewed by over one million households. He is happily married to his wife, Lauree, and is the proud father of two boys, Chad and Dustin.